AF569582

Louis Weber, CEO
Publications International, Ltd.
7373 North Cicero Avenue
Lincolnwood, Illinois 60712

Manufactured in China.

8 7 6 5 4 3 2 1

ISBN: 0-7853-6273-8

Library of Congress Control Number: 2001096920

CREDITS

Owners:
Special thanks to the owners of the cars featured in this book for their enthusiastic cooperation:

Cover Cars: Warren Boynton; David Piangerelli; Herman Seymour; Robert Yapell.

American Motors: Frank Burnham; Mick Cohen; David DeHaan.

Chrysler: Chris Davis; Alex H. Deeken; Ray and Anne Dolchanczyk; John Duffek. **Dodge:** Ray Banuls; Larry Barnett; Scott Brubaker; Chris Davis; Tom Devers. **Imperial:** Lawrence Pavia; Gene Satterfield. **Plymouth:** David Griebling; Aaron Kahlenberg; Rich and Kathy Krasowski; Fayegene and Rayma Rippelmeyer; Paul F. Schult; Jeff Wentz; Robert Yapell.

Ford: John Breda; Kim Cardin; Vince Cesena; Gary Dickinson; Rocky DiOrio; Cherie Jacobson; Tom Johnson; Christopher M. Krueger; Albert Schildknecht; Randall Skulemowski; Martin J. Vehstedt; Sam Wilson. **Lincoln:** Sherman Willams. **Mercury:** Ed Hickey; Greg Neffle; Jerry Robbin; Ron Russ.

General Motors: Buick: Keith and Wendy Horsfall; Albert A. Jones; Steve and Sally Kuss; Junior Markin; Susan and Horace Mennella; Keith J. Mueller. **Cadillac:** David Aiken; Ron Kendall; Ed Oberhaus. **Chevrolet:** Keith Duncan; Robert G. Finley; Dave and Mary Glass; Robert Kleckauskas; Jim MacDonald; Connie and Larry Mitchell; Frank Spittle; Charles E. Stinson; Steve Sydell; Phil Trifaro; Bill Worthington. **Oldsmobile:** Neil and Amber Matranga; Marc and LeAnn Schaub; David Yordi. **Pontiac:** Don Guskey; Bill Jr. and Lea Heutteman; Dave and Cindy Keetch; Mike and Jim Schaudek; Herman Seymour; Michael Vacik.

Studebaker: Stu Chapman; Mark Ward.

Imports: Adrian Braag; Jack Bernard Brown; Richard and Sydney Darnell; D. Herning; Charlene and Duane Hyatt; Tim John; Rich Kimball; Wayne Nelson; Phillippa Newman; David Piangerelli; Maury Richmond; Joseph Roach; Bob Sanov; Evelyn and John Willburn.

Miscellaneous: Tim Bargainer; Robert Landers; The William Lyon Collection; Ed McCoughlin; Alfred L. Olson; Joe Pollard; Pat Price.

Photography:
The editors gratefully acknowledge the cooperation of the following people who have supplied photography to help make this book possible:

Mike Baker; Scott Baxter; Ken Beebe; Joe Bohovic; Jan Borgfelt; Bart Bragg; Chan Bush; DaimlerChrysler Historical Collection; Mirco DeCet; Neil Doherty; Ford Photographic; GM Photographic; Thomas Glatch; David Gooley; Sam Griffith; Don Heiny; Bud Juneau; Milton Kieft; Dan Lyons; Vince Manocchi; Joe McHugh, California Highway Patrol Academy; Doug Mitchel; Mike Mueller; David Newhardt; NHRA Archives; Robert Nicholson; Nina Padgett; William J. Schintz; Tom Shaw; Richard Spiegelman; David Talbot; David Temple; Phil Toy; W.C. Waymack; Nicky Wright.

CONTENTS

FOREWORD

In 1965, pioneering consumer advocate Ralph Nader first gained national attention, with his book *Unsafe at Any Speed.* The controversial best-seller offered convincing evidence that auto manufacturers, in many cases, built cars with appalling designed-in dangers.

Some viewed the book as a shocking commentary on an arrogant industry too long unchecked by regulatory agencies. Others saw it as an unfair cheapshot at an important American institution. Regardless, Nader's efforts launched a movement that over the next decade would radically alter the ground rules of automotive engineering and design.

But the cars introduced for 1965 were conceived several years before then, in some cases originating in the late Fifties. Thus, Detroit's '65 offerings were a product of the same unfettered environment that had characterized the industry for decades. Designers and engineers were free to follow their whims with little meddling or constraint from the government—or anyone else, aside from corporate accountants.

Adding fuel to automakers' boldness during this time was a public hungrier than ever for a wider variety of models, greater luxury, and better performance. And average folks now had the money to pay for such pleasures—the U.S. economy was flying higher than ever, and unemployment was at record lows.

What resulted from this rare mix were among the most viscerally appealing cars of any era. Stylists had moved beyond the outrageous one-upmanship and chrome-dipped excess of the

Fifties, into an era in which clean, tasteful designs reigned supreme. At the same time, engineers were proving that these cars' simple, Fifties-era V-8 engines had plenty of room for development. Feeding buyers' nearly insatiable appetite for better performance, automakers steadily boosted power. Some, by 1965, were offering engines with more than double the output of those available ten years prior.

Nader and his followers vehemently pointed out that, like those of decades earlier, 1965 cars weren't very responsible in their use of materials, consumption of fuel, or protection of their occupants. And, in hindsight, those are points well worth noting.

But perhaps that devil-may-care attitude is what makes these machines so special. The 1965 model year was the beginning of the end for a time in which manufacturers were free to build the most tantalizing cars possible, without being restrained by the staggering array of obstacles that appeared in the years to come.

Those limitations, including tougher governmental regulations, brutal inflation, and several fuel crises, would conspire to end this swaggering, adventuresome period for Detroit. But the excitement and passion of the cars produced in that era will forever echo throughout the automotive landscape.

Welcome to the final act of the Golden Age.

1965

AMERICAN MOTORS COMPANY

RAMBLER

American Motors made a bold move in 1965. After years of carving out their niche as economy car specialists, AMC decided to take on the Big Three across the board, fielding models in all product categories. In some cases, the strategy worked well. Ambassador had a career year in '65, ringing up over 64,000 sales. Riding on a wheelbase stretched four inches to 116, the Ambassador offered chiseled, straight-edge styling. Notable was a fresh front design, with stacked quad headlights and a split-bar grille. Brightwork strips ran from nose to tail atop the fenders, and taillights wrapped around the rear to the side. Ambassador was offered in 880 and 990 trim, in a full range of bodystyles: a hardtop coupe, two- and four-door sedans, four-door wagons, and a convertible coupe. A 232-cid/155-hp six was standard under the hood. Optional was a 287-cid/198-hp six or a 327-cid/270-hp V-8.

The Rambler Classic returned in 550, 660, and 770 levels. Stylist Dick Teague took the existing 112-inch-wheelbase platform and penned a longer, squared-off look with design cues taken from the Ambassador. Two- and four-door sedans and four-door station wagons were offered, with the lowest priced model carrying a $2,142 sticker. Engine choices ranged from six to eight cylinders, 199 to 327 cid, 128 to 270 hp. Available optionally on either the 232 six or the V-8 engines was the wonderfully named Shift-Command Flash-O-Matic floor shifter. It allowed the driver to change gears manually (sans clutch) or leave it up to the transmission to decide. The Classic was also offered in a convertible version, for $2,696. It was one of no less than three ragtops offered by Rambler for the year (Ambassador and American, too) by the normally sensible-minded AMC. Unlike the Ambassador, Classic sales slipped in '65, a precursor of things to come.

The American arrived with two- and four-door sedan, two-door hardtop, and convertible offerings. 220, 330, and 440 trim levels were offered and prices ranged from $1,979 to 2,418. Styling carried over virtually intact from 1964's redo, save some bright-work and grille tweaks. The handsome front end still looked like a visual tribute to Chrysler's Turbine cars. Rambler's core compact, the American, took the prize for best gas mileage in the Mobil Economy Run and Pure Oil Performance Trials. The flathead 196-cid six carried over as standard running gear. The inline six made 90 hp in 220 and 330 Americans and 125 in 440 series cars. American buyers could also choose the new Torque Command 232-cid six, good for 145 hp in this application. Evidence of the Rambler campaign to replace stodgy with sporty was found inside and out. Flashy wire wheel covers were made available, and inside, floor shifters were optional for manual or automatic transmission cars.

Undoubtedly the most surprising news from Kenosha was the debut of the sporty Marlin fastback. Later in the decade, AMC would gain a certain notoriety for producing some very extroverted, good bang-for-the-buck muscle cars. But back in '65, people were still used to Rambler as a purveyor of sensible economy cars. Marlin (and the sporty cars that followed) made people adjust their thinking. Like a banker in a business suit who suddenly comes to work in a Hawaiian shirt and checkered slacks, the idea took a little getting used to. Rambler's customers were a conservative lot and many felt that AMC's attempts to expand market had abandoned them—and they went elsewhere.

The Marlin concept began as a showcar named the Tarpon, a flashy fastback designed by Richard Teague's studio. The Tarpon's tidy dimensions included a height of 50 inches and an overall length of 180 on a 106-inch wheelbase. Unfortunately, AMC Chief Roy Abernethy made the decision to stretch the production version from what had been a 2+2 coupe to an unprecedented 3+3 size slantback. As a result, Marlin was based on the Classic's platform, and the design expanded to fit the 112-inch wheelbase. History shows that many things have been put on the rack and pulled over the years, and that the results are usually unpleasant. Marlin was no exception. The slippery styling that had raised eyebrows for Tarpon on the show circuit was lost in its translation to production version. Marlin emerged as a rather ungainly looking coupe—longer, taller, and lacking in the better proportions that Tarpon's smaller size allowed. Standard power was provided by AMC's 287 V-8, with the 327 available as a step up. A three-speed manual was standard fare, with four-speed or automatic optional. Priced at $3,100, Marlin was Rambler's most expensive car for 1965. The big boattail sold 10,327 units in its rookie year (over twice as many as would sell in '66).

Marketed under the banner of "The Sensible Spectaculars," Rambler's overall sales were down for '65 and profits slipped, as retooling costs ate into the profit margin. Model year production of 391,366 was good for eighth industrywide—the same spot as they had occupied the year before.

1

AMC stepped up in class for 1965, abandoning their niche as economy-car specialists to do battle with the Big Three across the board. American, Classic, and Ambassador were small, medium, and large in the new, full-service menu. It was a big year for the biggest Rambler (Ambassador sold over 64,000 units), but less successful for the rest of the lineup, and overall, AMC remained eighth in model year production.

2

3

4

5

1. A handsome facelift helped Ambassador post a career year in sales in '65. 880 and 990 series were offered. The 880 four-door sedan (shown) was the second-best-seller in the Ambassador line, after the 990 four-door. 2. A 155-hp Torque Command Six was standard on Ambassadors like this 990 sedan, with optional 287-cid and 327-cid V-8s. 3. 990 Station Wagons were Rambler's upscale haulers for 1965. In addition, AMC offered an 880 series wagon, as well as models in the Classic and American series. Rooftop luggage rack was a no-cost extra on the 990, and options included third-row seating and simulated woodgrain side trim. 4. A look inside an Ambassador 880 four door. Road-Control power steering was an $84 option. Airliner reclining seats could be adjusted into seven positions. 5. Formal roofline was part of Ambassador's "Stately styling" for '65. 6. Two-tone paint scheme helped accentuate the crisp lines of the 990-H hardtop. 7. Rarest of the Ambassador 990s was the convertible; just 3,499 were produced.

6

7

1

Fully restyled for 1964, Rambler's American returned for '65 with minor cosmetic changes. "The compact economy king" was available in ten models covering three series.

2

1. Top hardtop was the 440-H. American had moved to a 106-inch wheelbase for '64. 2. Rambler advertising touted its most popular '65 model, the Ambassador. Stellar sales of the big Rambler doubled its previous best year. 3. Least expensive Rambler ragtop was the $2,418 American 440. It was the highest-priced car in the American series, and the lowest production model as well, with some 3,882 built. 4. Lift the hood on an American 440 and you would find one of two sixes: 196-cid/125-hp or 232-cid/155-hp. 5. Rambler's entry-level convertible could be dressed up with goodies like wire wheel covers, a power top, bucket seats, and two different kinds of floor shifts.

3

4

5

1

Rambler's intermediate lineup added a new player for 1965. A $2,696 convertible debuted in the top-line 770 series. Styling on all Classics was redone for '65, moving visually closer to the Ambassadors.

2

3

4

1. Rambler built 4,953 Classic 770 convertibles like this Frost White example in 1965. Five engines were available in the Classic series, ranging from the 199-cid/128-hp 1v Torque Command Six through a 327-cid/270-hp 4v V-8. Standard power top was offered in four colors: white, black, blue, and aqua. Five-spoke rims are not original for Classic. 2. Interior view of this 770 convertible shows standard vinyl upholstery, optional power brakes, and aftermarket steering wheel and sound system. 3. Said Rambler of its new Classic convertible, "Here is the vitality of youth—the promise of fresh air fun in a rock solid car that extends for 195 beautiful inches." 4. Cross Country four-door wagons were offered in 550, 660, and 770 trim. Rooftop luggage rack was standard, and additional storage was found in a hidden compartment beneath the rear deck. Rambler built 15,623 Classic 770 Cross Countrys like this one.

Marlin was the most obvious evidence of Rambler's efforts to go after the sporty-car market. Based on the Tarpon showcar and built on a bigger, Classic platform, Marlin made its debut for 1965 as a "3+3" fastback.

1

2

3

4

5

1. Marlin carried AMC's highest price tag ($3,100) and high hopes that the company could fish the same waters as Plymouth's Barracuda and Ford's Mustang; 10,327 sold in its inaugural year. 2, 3. Interior views of this Marlin show optional bucket seats fore and aft. Wide and sporty buckets cut seating capacity from 3+3 to 2+2, but still provided roomy seating for adults front or back, thanks to Marlin's stretched chassis and long roofline. 4. Marlin was a latecomer to the '65 lineup, arriving midyear. Rear views of the car were the most attractive and company advertisements heavily accented the back angles. 5. The tidy lines of the Tarpon show car are shown to good effect. Tarpon had been based on the American's smaller, 106-inch-wheelbase chassis. Stretching the production Marlin to ride on the 112-inch Classic wheelbase pulled the styling to ungainly proportions.

1965
1965
1965

CHRYSLER CORPORATION

CHRYSLER
DODGE
IMPERIAL
PLYMOUTH

You had to feel sorry for Plymouth's Barracuda. Born just a scant two weeks after Ford's famous ponycar, it was assumed to be a Mustang fighter. This was a case of mistaken identity, as Barracuda was designed with the Corvair Monza and Ford Falcon Sprint in mind. When the original targets disappeared from the market, Barracuda became a de facto ponycar, and in time a darn good one. But in 1965, Barracuda was newly spawned—and if this fish was cleaned, you'd find Valiant bones. Steps were being taken to up the fun quotient with the optional Formula S Package. It included a tachometer, a stiffer suspension with front antisway bar, wider wheels and tires, and a Commando 273-cid/235-hp V-8. So equipped, it made for a fairly fast fish, capable of 0-60 in eight seconds flat. Barracuda was popular in its sophomore year, notching 64,596 sales.

Compact Valiant was freshened with a new grille outside, while inside, pushbuttons were replaced by column or floor shifters. 100, 200, and Signet levels were available, ranging from $2,004 for a 100 series two-door sedan to $2,746 for a four-door 200 wagon.

Chrysler Corporation's brief early-Sixties experiment with downsizing its full-size cars was over in '65. Belvedere, formerly the "standard" Plymouth, was now an intermediate. A new model was added to the series—the sporty Satellite, available as a hardtop or convertible. Even sportier was the Satellite S/S. Offered as a two-door hardtop, it packed a 426 wedge with anywhere from 365 to 425 hp and cost $4,671.

Full size for Plymouth meant Fury, which rode into the new model year with fresh styling stretched over a longer chassis. The wheelbase gained three inches to 119 (121 on wagons). Fury's new look included what was fast becoming an industry staple—stacked, quad headlights. Four series were offered: Fury I, II, III, and Sport Fury. Fury III was the top seller, at 139,344 units.

To meet the needs of its diverse product line, Plymouth engine choices were many and varied, starting with the 225-cid slant Six and including 318, 383, and 426 V-8s. Like most automakers, Plymouth had a fine sales year in '65. Production of 728,228 was up a whopping 32 percent over the previous year and kept Plymouth firmly in fourth place overall, gaining on number three Pontiac and putting some ground between itself and number five Buick.

Unlike Plymouth, Dodge sales slipped for the year. Production of 489,065 cars was good enough for seventh industrywide, a notch below '64 levels. Dodge's full-size Polara and Custom 880s sported a new "dumbbell" grille and "delta" taillights. The big Dodges (back once again from Mopar's downsizing experiments) added a new linemate—a luxury sport coupe named Monaco.

Also added to the lineup was a new intermediate named Coronet, ready to do battle with Ford's Fairlane and Chevy's Chevelle. Able to compete with *anything*, at least on the track, was another Coronet—the limited production Hemi-Charger. A two-door sedan built on a shortened, 115-inch wheelbase (normal Coronet sedans ran 117), the Hemi-Charger was powered by a 426 Hemi, conservatively rated at 425 hp. Created to assault drag strips, the Hemi-Charger had a heavy-duty suspension, beefed-up brakes, and sub-seven-second 0-60 mph capability.

Other Dodge powerplant choices ranged from 170- and 225-cid slant sixes, through V-8s of 273, 318, 361, 383, 413, and 426 cid.

Dodge's compact Dart was starting its third year wearing a mild facelift that added a handsome checked grille up front and elliptical taillights in back. The side view showed off three "portholes," mounted low on the front fenders. A partial vinyl roof was a new option. Three series were offered: 170, 270, and a sporty GT hardtop. The latter listed for $2,404 with standard slant six, but could be had with a trio of 273-cid V-8s making up to 235 hp. Coupled to the newly available four-speed manual transmission, Dart's low 2,700 curb weight made it a peppy performer.

In midyear 1964, Dodge introduced its new compact A100 pickups, which continued for '65. When the company offered its 273-cid/174-hp V-8 in the A-series trucks, it became the first manufacturer to offer eight-cylinder power in a compact pickup. The V-8 joined 170- and 225-cid sixes as the other powerplant options. Dodge was intent on capturing a larger share of the pickup camper market in '65 and so the A100s were revised to improve their receptivity to slide-in campers.

Rounding out the light-truck offerings were D100 half tons—D200 three-quarter tons, and D300 one tons, as well the W-series 4×4s. The wheelbase on D and W series trucks was stretched to 128 inches for '65, allowing better weight distribution. A new eight-foot box increased cargo capacity and a full-length, 65-inch-wide tailgate made for easier access. Double wall side construction in the pickup box added durability. The new-design trucks got a fresh face as well, with big-bezeled, single headlights framing a wide-checked grille with inset parking lights. Out back, thinner, vertical lamps combined tail, brake, and directional lights in one unit and replaced the former round lenses. Interiors were spruced up with brighter, plusher materials. Like the compact trucks, all D and W series pickups were offered with the 273-cid V-8.

Since 1955, Chrysler's exclusive 300 series was marked each year by a different alphabetic designation. In 1965, the series was up to the letter "L." However, this could be interpreted "L" as in "Last," with this being the final year of letter-car status for Chrysler's elegant brutes. The 300L previewed the transition from executive hot rod to luxury offering. Future 300s were a less-exclusive breed. Under the hood of the 300L, power was provided by a 413-cid/360-hp V-8—relatively tame by letter-car standards but far from a stone. Always a limited production car, the 300L registered just 2,845 sales in '65, of which 440 were convertibles.

The 300, like all the '65 Chryslers, enjoyed new styling. Borrowing from the Imperial, these big Mopars had a handsome, linear look. The New Yorker was offered in five models and sold a little over 30,000 units. Newport was by far the biggest seller in the lineup. The seven models tallied a total of 125,795. Engine choices throughout the Chrysler line included a 383-cid V-8 ranging from 270-315 hp to a 413 that packed anywhere from 340-360 hp.

Overall, Chrysler had a fine year sales-wise in '65. The 206,089 units compared to just 153,319 one year earlier, though its overall place industrywide remained tenth.

Imperial for '64 had taken on a continental look, due to the influence of designer Elwood Engel. Engel was previously employed at Lincoln, where he had helped shape the striking Continental models that debuted in 1961. Returning for the fourth year of its styling cycle, Imperial carried forward with only slight changes. A new front-end look featured horizontal, quad headlights behind glass panels, and a four-quadrant grille. With a long 129-inch wheelbase, four models were offered: Crown hardtop coupe, sedan, and convertible were produced, ranging in price from $5,772 for the Crown hardtop sedan. In addition, a LeBaron hardtop sedan was offered at $6,596. With the exception of a handful of limos, the convertible was the rarest of the '65 Imperials, with just 633 built.

CHRYSLER

NEW YORKER

1

Credited to design chief Elwood Engel, the fully restyled, smoothly squarish 1965 Chryslers were a little shorter than before, but just as spacious inside. All wheelbases grew to 124 inches. Chrysler division's four-model output set a record, topping 206,000 cars.

2

3

4

5

1. Of the four models in Chrysler's 1965 lineup, the New Yorker led in poshness but not in sales. 2, 3. In addition to the $4,161 hardtop coupe, the New Yorker group included a hardtop sedan, town sedan, and a pair of Town & Country wagons. The 413-cid V-8 was rated 340 hp, with 360 horses optional. 4, 5. Top seller was the more modest Newport line, but only 3,192 convertibles went to customers, priced at $3,442. Newports used a 383-cid V-8 with four-barrel carburetor, rated at 270 or 325 hp. Pushbutton TorqueFlite transmissions were gone, replaced by a regular column-mounted gearshift.

1

Each year since 1955, Chrysler had offered a "letter-series" 300, serving as the division's sporty concoction. This season's 300L was destined to be the last warrior. Subsequent 300s would be toned-down in power and pizzazz.

2

3

4

5

6

1. Like its Chrysler mates, the 300L earned a linear restyling for 1965, reminiscent of the Imperial. 2. Front bucket seats and a long console greeted 300L occupants. Chrysler also offered a "plain" 300 series, aimed more at the family trade. 3. Only 440 300L convertibles were built, priced at $4,618. 4. Driving a full-size car in 1965 included the convenience of an abundantly sized trunk. 5. Though less potent than past 300 models, the 413-cid V-8 in the 300L whipped up a satisfying 360 horses. 6. Only two 300L body styles were available: hardtop coupe and convertible.

DODGE

Dodge's new midsize model revived the Coronet nameplate, and could be equipped with a mild-mannered six or a small-block V-8. Coronets could also carry V-8s as big as 426-cid, packing 365 hp, to satisfy the seriously power hungry.

1

2

3

4

5

6

1. Sport-minded buyers could gravitate toward the stylish, line-topping Coronet 500, marketed as a hardtop convertible or a $2,894 convertible, with bucket seats and a floor-shift console. 2. A civilized road machine, the Coronet 500 had a choice of seven V-8s, starting with a 273-cid/180-hp. 3. Like its regular mid-size Coronet companions, the 500 featured a square-cut profile. 4. A total of 32,745 Coronet 500s were produced for 1965—hardtop coupes and convertibles. 5. Dodge marketed an appetizing selection of lightweight body components for racing. 6. A Coronet 440 station wagon could seat either six or nine passengers.

Now in its third season, Dodge's compact Dart enjoyed a modest facelift for '65 that imparted a slightly more aggressive appearance. That change was especially welcome to buyers of the sporty Dart GT. Most Darts, though, saw service for family transportation, as did their Ford Falcon and Chevy II competitors. Hardtops could be fitted with a newly optional partial vinyl roof.

1

2

1. Dart buyers seeking a taste of sportiness in 1965 could be tempted by a red GT convertible, priced at $2,628.
2. Mild restyling of the compact Dart included new elliptical taillights and a checkered grille, as well as triple "portholes" sitting low on front fenders. A four-speed manual transmission could now be installed in the GT, raising its status among enthusiastic drivers. 3. In two-door hardtop form, the Dart GT stickered for $2,404 with the standard 170-cid Slant Six. A step-up 225-cid, 145-hp six-cylinder engine cost extra.
4. Far more fitting in the Dart GT was one of the 273-cid V-8s, putting out 235 hp when breathing through a four-barrel carburetor. 5. A stylized insignia let other drivers know that the seemingly family-oriented Dart was actually a GT edition, perhaps packing a hot V-8 beneath its hood. Production for 1965 totaled 45,116 Dart GT hardtops and convertibles.

3

4

5

1

2

In addition to redesigning all of its full-size models for 1965, Dodge launched a new Monaco two-door hardtop to compete against Pontiac's personal-luxury Grand Prix coupe.

If the standard 383-cid V-8 wouldn't quite suffice, buyers had a choice of two bigger "wedgehead" engines: a 413-cid V-8 rated at 340 hp, or 426-cid that unleashed 365 horses.

3

4

5

1. Front-end appearance of the new $3,355 Monaco hardtop coupe was nearly identical to that of Dodge's companion full-size Custom 880 and Polara series, led by a "dumbbell" shaped grille made up of slim vertical bars. Instead of the usual hood ornament, Monacos wore a tiny name tag. 2. Stylists began with a "clean sheet" to redesign Dodge's full-size models on a 121-inch wheelbase, following the lead of design chief Elwood Engel. Monacos came only in the hardtop coupe body style, with 13,096 built. 3. A bright panel stretched across the rear of the Monaco, between its "delta" trapezoidal taillights. 4. Only four passengers fit inside a full-size Monaco, due to the full center console, which contained a floor lever for the automatic transmission. 5. Bucket seats were becoming a perceived necessity in sport-oriented automobiles, even those with full-size exterior dimensions. Rattan wicker accents helped give the Monaco's upper door panels and seatbacks a distinctive appearance.

As directed by Elwood Engel, the 1965 redesign gave all Dodge full-size models a conservative, squarish appearance—with distinct details to attract the eye. Dodge toured the auto-show circuit with cutaway versions to demonstrate the engineering features of its full-size lineup.

1

2

3

4

5

1. Most Custom 880 models were mild and modest, created to provide reliable, if uninspiring, daily service for American families. Not so this Custom 880 convertible, which happens to house a 426-cid "street wedge" V-8 with dealer-installed dual carburetors and a four-speed floor shift. 2. Because full-size Dodges could be purchased with modest interiors and strong V-8 engines, they gained favor with police departments around the country. The Polara Police Pursuit sedan could have either a 383- or 413-cid V-8. Dodge also marketed a lightweight Police Patroller, based on the midsize Coronet. 3. A floor-mounted shifter operated the available four-speed manual gearbox in a Custom 880. Most full-size Dodges had an automatic transmission with a column-mounted lever. 4. Dodge dealers offered a half-dozen convertibles, including the $3,335 Custom 880, which had a standard 383 V-8, rated at 270 hp. 5. Fold-down armrests made the Custom 880 convertible most appealing for four occupants, despite the use of bench seats. A total of 44,496 Custom 880 models were built, versus just 12,705 full-size Polaras.

IMPERIAL

Considered a separate brand, Imperial led the Chrysler pack in luxury—and also in price. Front-end reworking for '65 featured glass-enclosed headlights. Four models were available. Although sales were respectable for an expensive luxury automobile, Imperial lagged well behind Cadillac and Lincoln in the mid Sixties.

1

2

3

4

1. Only 633 Imperial Crown convertibles were produced in 1965, priced at a then eye-popping $6,194. Interiors were plush but conventional, with separate seatbacks for the driver and front passenger. Judged by the American Automobile Association's roominess index, the Imperial's interior was the biggest in the industry. The Imperial's 413-cid V-8 developed 340 hp. 2. Restyled in 1964, adopting a sharper-edged profile that was slightly reminiscent of Lincoln's Continental, the Imperial showed only modest changes this season. The subtle spare-tire hump incorporated into the trunklid was an Imperial hallmark. 3. New horizontal quad headlights sat behind glass panels, flanking a fresh four-quadrant grille with a mesh background. Bestseller for '65 was the Crown hardtop sedan, with 11,628 units built and a $5,772 price. 4. Topping the regular-production Imperial series was the LeBaron four-door hardtop, priced at $6,596. Only 2,164 were produced. Total Imperial volume dropped by nearly 5,000 units, to 18,409 in all, and would decline further yet in 1966. Only ten final examples of the ultra-posh, stretched Ghia Crown Imperial went on sale, produced in Spain and sold for a whopping $18,500 apiece.

1

Mounting a fastback coupe superstructure atop the everyday Valiant chassis yielded the Barracuda, sending Plymouth into the sporty compact realm. Though introduced only a couple of weeks after Ford's Mustang, as a "1964½" model, the two were never serious rivals.

2

3

4

5

6

1. Blending a lightweight body and a hot V-8 engine made the Barracuda attractive to enthusiasts, even if it fell short of the Mustang league. Barracudas ranked closer to Corvair Monzas and Falcon Sprints. A "Formula S" edition of the Barracuda arrived for '65, equipped with such extras as a firmer suspension, front antisway bar, and wider tires. 2. Folded-down back seats were rare in Detroit-built automobiles, giving Barracuda buyers a cargo deck that measured seven feet long. 3. Easy-to-spot styling touches included a massive wraparound rear window. 4. Despite the Barracuda's fastback profile and huge rear glass, it had a conventional, if stubby, trunklid. 5. Base engine was a 145-hp slant six, but Barracudas could contain a 273-cid V-8 that made 180 hp. Wilder yet was the 235-hp "Commando" V-8 that propelled the Formula S. 6. A tachometer was part of the Formula S package.

Brand-new styling for 1965 turned the formerly shrunken Fury into a true full-size automobile. Crisp body lines gave the popular family car an almost formal appearance. Four new well-equipped series went on sale: Fury I, II, and III, plus the aptly named Sport Fury hardtop coupe and convertible.

1

2

3

4

5

6

7

1. Rather posh fittings helped make the Fury III Plymouth's top-selling full-size series, with 139,344 built, despite its higher prices. Standard engine was a 318-cid V-8, but this four-door hardtop packs a 383. 2. Not only was the 1965 Fury III the biggest Plymouth ever, it was also the roomiest. 3. The Fury's optional 383-cid V-8 developed either 270 or 330 hp. 4. Fury models rode a longer, 119-inch wheelbase and displayed a blockier physique. Unibody construction continued, but a bolt-on subframe held the engine and front suspension. 5, 6. Fury III models came in five body styles, including this two-door hardtop that stickered for $2,691. 7. On its handsome horizontally themed dashboard, the Fury's speedometer was flanked on the left by three gauges, and on the right by climate controls, radio, and clock.

1

1. No ordinary Sport Fury, this flag-bedecked white ragtop served as a Parade Car at the 1965 Indianapolis 500 race, which was paced by a Sport Fury. Beneath its hood sat a 426-cid V-8 engine, ready to unleash a potent 365 hp. 2. A 318-cid V-8 was standard in the Sport Fury, but choices included a pair of 383s as well as the non-Hemi 426, yielding performance to match the shapely lines. 3. A total of 6,272 Sport Fury convertibles were built, along with 38,348 hardtop coupes. Styling resembled that of the Fury III, except for minor trim differences. 4. Offered only in hardtop coupe and convertible form, the full-size Sport Fury featured an all-vinyl interior with the expected bucket seats, alongside a center console that held a floor lever for the TorqueFlite automatic transmission.

2

OFFICIAL
Plymouth
PACE CAR
·FORTY-NINTH ANNUAL INDIANAPOLIS 500 MILE RACE·MAY 31, 1965·
INDY 65

3

4

Once known as sensible but stodgy family cars, Plymouths went racing in the Sixties. Sizzling big-block V-8s teamed with stripped-down, lightweight, midsize bodies to create captivating power-to-weight ratios for competition at the nation's drag strips.

1

2

3

1. Plymouth's 426-cid Max Wedge V-8 engine powered this altered-wheelbase Fury A/FX drag car, shown with its hood removed. Instead of the Wedge, Plymouth could provide racing teams with a "Super Commando" Hemi V-8. Conservatively rated at 425 hp it was ready for NASCAR or dragstrip duty.
2. This particular Fury A/FX drag car is equipped with a selection of later-model aftermarket engine parts, special wheels, and other modifications. 3. Note the massive rear overhang on the A/FX hardtop coupe, which participated in drag racing as a "Golden Commando" team car. 4. Structural revisions for A/FX drag racing included moving the battery from its usual spot under the hood to a location in the trunk space. 5. This shortened-wheelbase "Golden Commandos" Plymouth drag car competed under the auspices of Hamilton Motors, in Detroit.

4

5

1

Plymouth launched a sporty Satellite midsize hardtop coupe and convertible for 1965, equipped with bucket seats and packing V-8 power. All intermediates, including the Belvedere I and II, were reskinned to resemble the big Fury and dubbed the "new midsize."

2

3

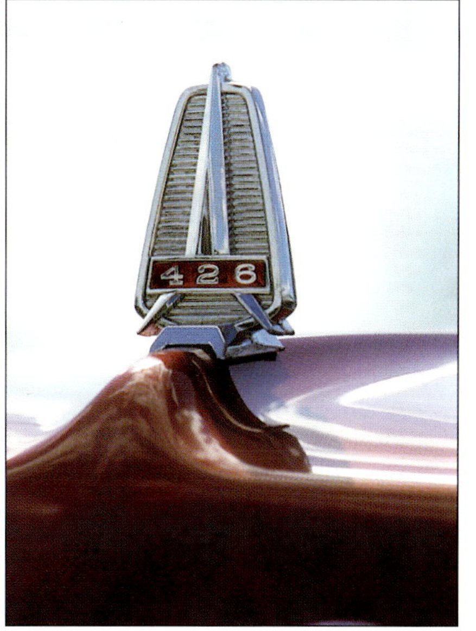

5

1. Satellites came only in two-door hardtop and convertible body styles, whereas the Belvedere I and Belvedere II had a broader range. Brisk Satellite sales totaled 6,272 convertibles and 38,348 hardtops. 2. Bucket-style seats in the Satellite flanked a long center console, which contained the selector lever for the TorqueFlite automatic transmission. 3. Standard engine in the Satellite was a 318-cid V-8, but this example benefits from the big 426-cid engine, rated at 365 hp. 4. Midsize Plymouths, including this soft-topped Satellite, rode a 116-inch wheelbase. 5, 6. A "426" hood ornament and "Commando V-8" insignia left no doubt about the power source lurking under a Satellite's hood.

6

4

1

Kin to the Dodge Dart, Plymouth's compact Valiant adopted a fresh grille for 1965. Valiants came in three price levels: base 100, midrange 200, and premium Valiant Signet, the latter offered only as a bucket-seat hardtop coupe and convertible.

2

3

4

1. Plymouth's least-expensive convertible was the compact Valiant 200, priced at a modest $2,437. Low cost wasn't enough to attract boatloads of buyers, however. Only 2,769 of the convertibles rolled off the line. 2. A column-mounted gearshift lever replaced pushbutton selectors for the Valiant's optional TorqueFlite automatic transmission. Valiants had a standard three-speed manual gearbox, with four-speed floor-shift optional. 3. Slant six engines were standard, but the Valiant 200 got a 225-cid version, while the 100's six was only 170-cid. A 273-cid V-8 (shown) was optional in the 200 series, developing 180 hp with a two-barrel carburetor or 235 hp with a four-barrel. 4. Valiant 100s were upholstered in vinyl, with standard front-seat armrests. 5. A Valiant 100 four-door sedan, with 170-cid Slant Six and column-shifted three-speed manual transmission, was about as basic as a domestic car could get in 1965.

5

1965

FORD MOTOR COMPANY

FORD
LINCOLN
MERCURY

By the time the calendar flipped to 1965, Ford's '65 Mustang had already been out of the paddock for about nine months. From its official debut at the New York World's Fair on April 17, 1964, through the end of model year 1965, Mustang sold an astounding 680,989 units. That total included 101,945 convertibles, which were offered for $2,614. Also in that tally were some 77,000 fastback models. The sleek, 2+2 body style was added to the lineup in the fall of '64. Mustang was the product of a host of Ford designers, planners, and marketers, along with its top proponent Lee Iacocca. Shortly thereafter, Iacocca was promoted to Vice President of Ford's Car & Truck Group.

Mustang's magic had three primary components. First was the long hood/short deck style that quickly became known as the "ponycar" look. A second key was a long-as-your-arm options list that allowed buyers to spec their cars as anything from mild to wild. The final ingredient of Mustang's success was its lack of true rivals. It wasn't really until 1967 when real competitors appeared, in the form of the Camaro, Firebird, and the second-generation Barracuda.

Mustang's horsepower was supplied by two engines initially. A 170-cid/101-hp six was standard, replaced in fall 1964 by a 200-cid/120-hp six. At first, the optional powerplant was a 260-cid V-8, but that was succeeded in late 1964 by a 289 that could be had in versions ranging from 200 to 271 hp.

If the Ford Falcon thought the Mustang ungrateful, it could be forgiven. Falcon, which had donated its chassis to the high flying Mustang, rolled into 1965 with just a minor facelift, one year after getting a major squared-off restyle. Sales of the sportier Sprint convertible and hardtop versions suffered at the hands of the newcomer. Less than 7,000 sold in '65, compared to 20,000 plus in '64.

Thunderbird emerged with minor cosmetic changes—it, too, had been restyled for '64. A new grille and wheel covers were added, and a reverse C-spear design appeared on front fenders. A T-Bird emblem replaced the former block letters along the leading edge of the hood. Front disc brakes became standard equipment and stylish, sequential triple taillights made their debut. With a base sticker price of $4,486, T-Bird sales dipped below 75,000 for the year.

Midsize Fairlane received a mild reskin and rode a wheelbase stretched a half-inch longer than that of the '64. The standard 200-cid six was now rated at 120 hp and there were three V-8 options. Fairlane sales were also off from previous levels, measuring 223,954 for '65.

Galaxie was the happy recipient of a full makeover for 1965, with new, square-shoulder styling. Stacked, quad headlights flanked a full-length grille in front, while the rear lighting went from round to semirectangular thanks to restyled hexagonal taillights on most models. Sporty and upscale variants were offered in the XL and LTD. The latter caused a bit of a PR stir with an ad campaign that proclaimed it, "…quieter than a Rolls-Royce." Galaxie ran a standard six-cylinder engine, with a half-dozen optional

V-8 offerings. Despite the smart new looks, Galaxie sales slipped in a bull car market, forecasting an upscale move in buyer preferences.

The big news for Ford's F-series light trucks was new Twin I-Beam front suspension. Although it was more of a swing-axle design than a true independent suspension, it was nonetheless a marked improvement over the previous beam-axle. At the same time, a mild restyle brought a new grille with repositioned parking lights. Engine choices now included the standard 240-cid/150-hp six, optional 300-cid/170-hp six and 352-cid/208-hp V-8. Light truck sales for the year tallied 563,137.

Like Galaxie, Mercury's full-size models were restyled for '65, and rode a 123-inch wheelbase. Three inches longer than previous models, the big Mercs had straight lines with Lincolnesque styling cues. A stiffer body and chassis structure resulted in a quieter ride. Three series, 15 models, and six rooflines were offered. Included in that roster were the unusual Breezeway sedans, which had a backward sloping rear window. The Monterey series offered six models, starting at $2,767. Montclair was next up, with three models and a base sticker of $3,135. The top of the class was Park Lane, with four offerings, starting at $3,267 and a convertible model priced at $3,599. Big Mercurys came with standard 390-cid/250-hp V-8, and choices ran all the way up to an optional 427-cid/410-hp V-8.

Comet sported a fresh facelift that included stacked headlights and a red-white-and-blue grille center piece. Shades of Buick, the front fenders sprouted rectangular portholes. The revamped rear design featured wedge shaped, wraparound taillights. Model offerings stayed the same for the Merc compact: 202, 404, Caliente, and Cyclone. Another likely casualty of the Mustang effect, Comet sales sagged for '65—the only Mercury model to do so. Overall production hit 346,751 for the year, an increase of 14 percent over 1964 and good for ninth place, industrywide.

Luxury linemate Lincoln entered '65 on the fourth year of its styling cycle, and the deft '61 makeover of the Continental was wearing well. Lincolns now sported a slight hood bulge; a flatter grille; and wraparound, ribbed parking lights and taillamps. In a move with little known logic, the convertible top mechanism for '65 Lincolns was different from both the earlier models and those that followed it. Two hydraulic pistons were mounted directly in the trunk, presenting an obstacle to luggage storage space on soft tops.

Less controversial was the addition of standard front disc brakes and seat belts. More fabric choices were available for the interior and a vinyl roof was added to the options list as well.

Mechanix Illustrated's venerable Tom McCahill tested a '65 Continental convertible. He liked the added stopping power of the new brakes but disliked the loss of storage space in the ragtop's trunk. McCahill recorded a top speed of 111 mph, with a 0-60 mph best of 11.1 seconds. Buyers certainly liked what they saw—Continental sales were up almost 4,000 units for the year, at 40,180.

Ford racing fans had much to be happy about in '65, though the division's dominance carried a pronounced asterisk—Chrysler boycotted virtually the entire race year. Ford won 48 of 55 NASCAR Grand National races, with Ford driver Ned Jarrett taking the championship. Also, Jim Clark's Ford powered Lotus won the Indy 500, the first rear-engine car to do so.

1

Despite a facelift aimed at mirroring the Galaxie's clean, clipped lines, Fairlane production dipped to a record low 223,954 units in 1965.

2

3

1. Since the first Fairlane midsize models appeared in 1962, yearly design tweaks had gradually squared off the body lines. 1965's reskin finished the job. The ¾ back angle was arguably the most successful view. 2. Chrome horn ring, window moldings, and armrests fore and aft mark this interior as that of the uplevel Fairlane 500. 3. In the last year of the styling cycle, Fairlane took on a sheet-metal resemblance to its big brother Galaxie. The wheelbase was stretched a half-inch, and length, width, and weight were all up slightly. Engine choices included the standard, 200-cid/120-hp six as well as a trio of 289 V-8s. Prices ranged from $2,230 to $2,648.

1. A Fairlane two-door sedan like this one stickered for $2,230 and some 13,685 were produced. 2. At the opposite end of the model price spectrum were the Fairlane 500 station wagons, which retailed for $2,648. Four-door wagons were offered in both Fairlane and Fairlane 500 trim. Profile view of the latter *(right)* shows off a chrome body side strip with aluminum insert. 3. Model name callout on Fairlane's front fenders was replaced by full-length side spear on 500s. 4, 5. As shown in the interior shots of this '65 Fairlane 500 wagon, carpeting replaced the vinyl mats used on base Fairlanes. This car's owner has augmented the standard dash display with several after-market gauges.

1

2

3

4

5

1

Falcon's sporty line leaders—Futura Sprint hardtop and convertible—were caught in Mustang's huge shadow, so their sales sputtered in '65. Both models didn't return for 1966. Sprints aside, Falcon and Futura trim levels differed little in looks from their '64 counterparts.

2

3

4

5

1. Front view of the Futura station wagon shows '65's new face. A simple, horizontal grille was bisected by a vertical bar, capped with a red-white-and-blue crest. 2. Distinguished by broad swaths of faux wood trim, the Squire wagon was the top of the line for Falcon's family haulers. It had a sticker price of $2,665, and just over 6,700 were built. 3. One step below the Squire was the Futura wagon, which listed for $2,506. Full-length spear with painted insert was a Futura exclusive. 4. Aftermarket wheel wrap helps this wagon's owner get a grip on the reins. 5. This Futura wagon is powered by Ford's 289-cid V-8—newly available in Falcon this year.

1

Ford's full-size models for '65 sported handsome new styling, with clean, subtle lines and modest ornamentation. The division boasted that the big cars were its "Newest since 1949."

2

3

1. As seen in this Galaxie 500/XL convertible, the crisp, linear lines of Ford's full size '65s looked good coming and going. Visible from this view are the hexagonal taillights, which replaced Ford's trademark round rear lenses on all but the Custom and Custom 500 series cars (and related wagons). 2. Standard bucket seats and floor-mounted shifter marked the interior of the 500/XL. Note the dressy bright trim on door panels and seat frames. 3. Though the 289-cid V-8 was standard on XLs, many owners opted for one of the two optional 390-cid Thunderbird V-8's (shown). 300- and 330-hp versions were offered as well as a potent 425-hp 427. 4. Stacked, quad headlights flanked the broad, beveled grille.

4

1

1. Plush LTD was the new top trim level of the Galaxie 500 series. Buyers went for luxury in a big way in '65, and 37,691 drove home in an LTD hardtop. 2. Interior view of LTD shows the couchlike comfort of the bench seating. 3. 500/XL and LTD hardtops kept the semifastback roofline of previous generation cars. 4. LTD's four-door sedan sold 68,038 units in '65. Ford raised a lot of eyebrows with an advertising campaign in which three Rolls-Royce chauffeurs claimed that LTD was quieter than a Rolls.

2

3

4

1

1. Sleek, semifastback roofline gave the 500XL hardtop a slippery profile on the street, and made it the body style of choice for Ford's stock car program. For car buyers, however, sport was losing favor to luxury in 1965, and production of the 500XL coupe slid over 48 percent, to 28,141. 2, 3. Nicely creased sheetmetal and formal roofline looked sharp on the Galaxie 500 four-door sedan—the sales stalwart among the big Fords. The '65 edition sold 181,183 units, at an MSRP of $2,678. A 240-cid/150-hp six-cylinder engine was standard equipment, with a raft of optional V-8s available. 4. Abbreviated chrome side molding identifies this as a Custom 500 model—the top trim level of the base Custom series. Sales of Custom 500 four-door sedans like this one were up ever so slightly over 1964 levels (71,727 vs. 68,828). 5. The entry-level offering for Ford's full-size lineup was the Custom 2-door sedan. Note round taillights in rectangular housing.

2

3

4

5

1

Mustang got a jump on the ’65 model year with its spring 1964 launch. In 1965, Mustang grew into a genuine sales sensation. On top of 121,538 early “1964½” sales, Ford’s trick pony galloped out of the showroom and into an additional 559,451 driveways in model year 1965.

2

3

4

1, 2. Mustang's long-hood/short-deck styling was so popular that it established a whole new auto category—ponycars—and spawned a rash of imitators. In addition to the clean, sporty design, key to Mustang's success was its long options list. With it, buyers could personalize their ponycar. 3. The slick looking, fastback 2+2 body style didn't join the hardtop and convertible models until autumn of 1964. Though priced close to the ragtop, it sold over 77,000 units in '65. 4. Fastbacks traded their rear quarter windows for a set of louvered, air extractor vents. The sloped roofline made for cramped quarters in back, but the rear seat folded forward to act as a parcel shelf.

1. Sun worshipers embraced the Mustang convertible in record numbers. Priced at $2,614, some 101,945 were sold between the midyear introduction and the end of model year 1965. 2. A look inside this Mustang's insides reveals many popular options. Included in this list are the Rally-Pac gauges and Instrument Group (tach and clock astride the steering column, four gauges flanking the round speedometer), deluxe steering wheel, push-button radio, center console, and Cruise-O-Matic automatic transmission. 3. Hard to resist the good looks of Ford's hot little convertible and as history records, few people did. 4. Embossed horses in the seat backs came to be known as the "pony" interior. 5. The famous galloping Mustang took center stage in the honeycomb grille.

1

2

3

4

5

1

In the second year of its fourth generation, the ’65 Thunderbird looked much like the ’64. T-Bird tallied just under 75,000 copies in ’65, against 92,465 in 1964.

2

3

4

1. Rarest 'Bird of all '65s was the Limited Edition Special Landau. An option package on the Landau model, the Limited Edition included "Ember-Glo" metallic paint, a parchment colored vinyl top, and other goodies. Though priced at just $50 more than the standard Landau, only 4,500 were built. 2. With a full restyle for 1964, changes were few for '65. Most prominent in this picture are the simulated air vent "C-spears" on front fenders and new wheel covers. Hiding behind those hubcaps are standard front disc brakes. 3. A look inside at T-Bird's snazzy interior. Note the massive center console and "thin-shell" front seat design, adopted for 1964. 4. Front view of the new T-Bird shows restyled grille with six horizontal bars and T-Bird emblem, which replaced the former block lettering on the hood's lip.

LINCOLN

Lincoln marketed itself as, "America's most distinguished motorcar." The division played on the you-are-what-you-drive theory, with ads that asked the rhetorical question, "What does your car say about you?"

1

2

1. Slab sides and chiseled lines on the '65 Continental look supremely elegant. Safety was selling in 1965: Front disc brakes became standard equipment in Lincolns, seatbelts had been added in mid '64. 2. A rear view of the Continental convertible. Absent from '65 models was the grille appliqué that had formerly stretched between the taillights, mirroring the front end design. The taillights (like the front parking lights) now wore chrome grilles. 3. Three-quarter view shows revamped front grille, which bulged out in the center. Wraparound front parking lights harmonized with the taillights, giving the Continental nighttime side visibility, fore and aft.

3

MERCURY

1

Mercury's resident compacts and budding muscle cars came back from 1964's intro year cleaner—thanks to a tidier design—and meaner, courtesy of 15 additional hp in the Cyclone's standard 289 V-8.

2

1. Comet's '64 design got a deft freshening for '65. Mags, white-letter radial tires, and dash mounted tach are aftermarket add-ons. 2. Cyclone's standard 289 2v put out 200 hp. Optional was a 225-hp 4v Super Cyclone mill. *Motor Trend* went 0-60 mph in 8.8 seconds with the latter, and turned the quarter mile in 17.1. This car's owner has added Ford Cobra-style valve covers. 3. Buckets and console were standard equipment on Cyclones; Hurst shifter and gauges above and below dash are owner additions. 4. Over 165,000 Comets sold in 1965. 5. 12,347 of that total were Comet Cyclones. 6. The Caliente convertible was the sole Comet ragtop, which included standard power top. 7. For the '65 auto show season, Mercury commissioned famed customizer Gene Winfield to build this Comet Cyclone "Sportster." Among its many experimental features were pistol grips for steering, and touch pads instead of pedals for clutch, brakes, and accelerator.

3

4

5

6

7

1

Full-size Mercurys grew even more so for ’65. Larger bodies and Lincolnesque lines helped move 181,699 big Mercs. Mercury’s overall sales of 346,751 cars were its best ever, though the company’s market share improved only slightly over 1964 levels.

2

3

1. The entry-level Monterey was the best-selling big Mercury for '65. The six-model Monterey lineup included a two-door convertible, two- and four-door sedans, a four-door hardtop, four-door Breezeway, and the two-door hardtop, like this one. 2. Like the other big Mercs, this fastback hardtop rode on a new 123-inch-wheelbase chassis, three-inches longer than the previous platform. 3. The unique Breezeway roofline returned as an offering in Monterey, Montclair, and Park Lane series. Back-sloping rear glass included a power window that retracted for better air circulation. 4. 390-cid 2v V-8 was standard issue in Monterey models. It made 250 hp. Variations of the 390 powered all full-size Mercurys and could be had in versions ranging up to 330 hp. The most muscle available was the 425-hp 427. 5. Breezeway's distinctive roofline as found in Mercury's top-of-the-line Park Lane series. Aside from the prominent chrome rake on front fenders, big Mercurys had rather little bodyside trim.

4

5

1

1.Top of the line for Mercury was the handsome Park Lane convertible. The open air Park Lane stickered for $3,599, and sold 3,008 units. Mercury reserved the stoutest standard version of their 390-cid V-8 for Park Lane—it was rated at 300 hp. 2. The inviting interior of the '65 Park Lane convertible was available with leather bench seating for an additional $98.80. 3. Tail-end treatment of '65 full-size Mercs was miles apart from previous models. Lights went from triple-horizontal to dual-vertical design, and gone was the brightwork grille between them. 4. Mercury lured enough people into the driver's seat to edge past Rambler into eighth place in the industry's model year production.

2

3

4

GENERAL MOTORS

BUICK
CADILLAC
CHEVROLET
OLDSMOBILE
PONTIAC

Business was booming at Chevrolet in 1965. The Bow Tie brand recorded an industry leading 2,375,118 cars produced—their best sales year of the decade. Corvair's 1965 redesign made news both for what you could see and what you could feel. Deft new lines from GM styling gave the little Chevy a bit of European flair. Corvair's base engine for '65 made an anemic 95 hp in standard form, but ran up to 140 hp. For those who wanted more, the new Corsa model could be fitted with a turbocharger, which boosted power to 180 hp. So equipped, the rear-engine compact could scoot to a respectable 11-second 0-60 time. More importantly, all Corvairs were now riding on a fully independent rear suspension, which addressed long-standing concerns about the first-generation car's handling.

With new styling and improved mechanicals, Monza and Corsa sold well in '65, with over 200,000 units produced. However, its popularity would start to wane in 1966, which had less to do with a man named Nader than it did a horse named Mustang.

As conventional as Corvair was different, Chevy II continued for 1965 as a traditional compact Falcon fighter. A bare-bones two-door sedan with a 153-cid/90-hp four cost $2,011. At the opposite end of the Chevy II spectrum, the Nova Super Sport proved that any box could be made more appealing if you filled it with the right ingredients, in this case V-8 options ranging to 327/300. Alas, even with hotter performance versions, the Chevy II's plain but pleasant styling was not keeping pace with the competition, and sales dipped by 37 percent for the year.

Chevelle was slightly revamped for '65: a bit longer and lower, with new grille, bumper, and taillight designs. The intermediate became Chevy's standard bearer for the burgeoning muscle-car wars of the Sixties. Malibu SS models were available with up to 350 hp from the 327. A midyear addition to the hi-po troops was the Chevelle SS 396, available with 375 hp, and capable of six-second 0-60 times. Just 201 white-knuckled owners drove one home.

Full-size Chevys were treated to a restyle. A Super Sport version was offered, in a coupe for $2,839 and a soft top starting at $3,104. New to the lineup was Caprice. Launched in response to Ford's LTD, it was a $200 option based on the four-door Impala hardtop. With an interior dressed out in luxurious trim, Caprice also boasted suspension and chassis tweaks engineered to provide a smoother ride. Outside, a blackout grille and vinyl top, along with special badging, wheel covers, and rocker moldings identified the upscale new entry.

Corvette, meanwhile, was in the third year of arguably its finest design cycle ever. Visual cues for the model year included triple vertical louvers on the front fenders and the removal of the former hood depressions. Four-wheel disc brakes were now standard. Underhood, 1965 marked both a first and a last for Corvette. Newly available was the L78 396 V-8, the first big block ever to grace Corvette's engine compartment. An additional $293 bought 425 bone-rattling hp and 5.7-second 0-60 times. But 1965 was also the last year for the 'Vette's fuel injection, which wouldn't return to the lineup until 1982.

Midyear 1964, El Camino returned from hiatus, now based on the intermediate Chevelle platform. The pickup/car hybrid got a mild facelift for '65, with a horizontally bisected grille.

Year three for Buick's Riviera produced quite possibly the most handsome Riv yet. Stacked headlights were hidden behind vertical sliding shields. At the opposite end, taillights were recessed into the bumper. A 401/325 "Nailhead" V-8 was standard, with a 425/360 optional. A Gran Sport Edition was made available for both Riviera and Skylark this year. Five-spoke rims highlighted the exterior. A heavy-duty suspension and quicker steering allowed GS Riviera to walk the walk.

The Buick lineup included Special, Skylark, LeSabre, Electra 225, Wildcat, and Riviera. Among the possibilities were no less than five convertibles. Wagon choices were now two—LeSabre dropping out, Special and Skylark remaining.

Wildcat left the LeSabre's 123-inch wheelbase in favor of the Electra's stretched 126-inch platform. Skylark evolved from the top level of the Special series to become its own series. Looking cleaner for '65, the Skylark Gran Sport was Buick's hot entry in the intermediate muscle car sweepstakes.

For the year, Buick was fifth once again in production, though the overall numbers were up slightly from '64 (553,870 vs. 510,490).

One behind Buick in the industry rankings was Oldsmobile, inching up a spot over '64's showing. The F-85 was now a midsize, fully 10-inches longer and wearing a revamped grille, taillights, and trim. The 225-cid/155-hp Econ-O-Way engine was offered for the frugal and engine choices ran skyward from there. Late in '64, Olds joined the muscle car fraternity with its new 4-4-2. Available on any F-85 coupe or convertible, it featured a 345-hp, 400-cid V-8 underhood.

Full-size models were treated to a restyle, with new rooflines and more trunk room. A four-speed transmission was offered in all 88, Starfire, and Jetfire models for the first time, along with GM's new Turbo Hydra-Matic transmission.

The high-line station wagon with the unique skylight glass, Oldsmobile's Vista Cruiser made its debut for 1964. Continuing for '65, Vista Cruiser had a base sticker price of $2,937, and sales topped 5,000 units for the year.

As elsewhere in GM, Pontiac's full-size models drove into 1965 on new styling. Hardtops received a new, semifastback roofline. The exception was Grand Prix, which kept its '64 top profile and concave rear window, while gaining the same, wide haunch body style as the other big Ponchos. The new style measured a mere 1.6-inches longer than previous models, but the flared flanks made it look larger. Full-size Pontiacs also rode on the same GM-wide platform modifications. A full perimeter chassis replaced the former X-member design.

Pontiac's intermediates were carried over with mild modifications. The GTO continued as an option package for the Tempest LeMans. Changes were mostly those associated with the LeMans facelift: Headlights went from horizontal to vertical and taillights were incorporated into a ribbed panel that stretched the length of the rear deck. Power was up, too—the standard 389 was now rated at 335 hp thanks to reworked heads. The optional Tri-Power setup bumped it up further to 360. Triple-carb GTOs were capable of 0-60 runs in the low six-second range. GTO sales doubled in its second season, with over 75,000 units produced in 1965.

Pontiac had its best sales year to date in '65, with the third-best production total of all automakers. *Motor Trend* magazine awarded the 1965 Car of the Year award to the entire Pontiac lineup.

Cadillac's handsome '65 models contained a styling surprise. The sharply creased lines were the first since 1948 not to sport tailfins. Four headlights flipped from '64's horizontal position to a vertical outlook and flanked a clean, contoured grille with inset parking lights. Eleven models were offered in five series, stretched over three separate wheelbases. Series 62 was renamed Calais this year. Pillared sedans replaced hardtops in all four-door models.

GM chassis improvements were found under the skin. A box-section perimeter frame replaced the former X-member design, and suspension fore and aft was modified to reduce dive and squat. The result: more stability, less noise, and a smoother ride.

Cadillac's 429-cid V-8 now breathed through a "sonically balanced" exhaust, tuned to provide a more mellifluous tone. Though buff books were not apt to wring out luxury models, one magazine reported a 0-60 time of 8.5 seconds for the two ton plus Cadillac, with a 16.4 quarter mile.

With crisp new styling and prices barely increased from previous levels, it was no surprise that Cadillac sold a company record 182,435 cars—three times more than Lincoln and Imperial combined.

BUICK

All full-size General Motors models, including the big Buicks, gained a more rounded appearance with their 1965 restyling. Luxury leader was again the Electra 225, offered in four body styles and regular or Custom trim, on a 126-inch wheelbase.

1

2

3

4

1. Two-door hardtops were the least popular members of the plush Electra 225 lineup. A 401-cid/325-hp V-8 engine was standard, but an optional 425-cid V-8 could yield either 340 or 360 hp. 2. The Electra 225 pillared four-door sedan came in either standard or Custom dress. 3. Buick offered five distinct convertibles for 1965, including the midsize Special and Skylark, bigger LeSabre, and full-size Wildcat and Electra 225. A ragtop Skylark GS raised the total to an even half-dozen. Most costly Buick of them all was the Electra 225 Custom convertible, priced at $4,440. 4. Four-door hardtops turned out to be the best-selling Electra 225 models in 1965. Buick also offered a Wildcat series on the same wheelbase, and LeSabres on a 123-inch span.

Shoppers who savored the size of a big Buick, but preferred a little more sportiness, could turn to the 10-model Wildcat series, which moved to the Electra 225's longer (126-inch) wheelbase this year.

1

2

3

1. Produced in base or Deluxe trim, the four-door sedan was one of four Wildcat body styles. Three of the bodies were offered in top-line Custom trim. As a result of switching from the LeSabre's wheelbase to that of the Electra 225, the 1965 Wildcat stretched to more than 219 inches overall. 2. Wildcat two-door hardtops came in three trim levels. The sloped roofline of its smooth new, less-angular body made the Wildcat look especially sleek and swift. 3. Pillared four-door sedans were not the strongest sellers in the Wildcat group, beating only the more expensive convertible. Pillarless hardtop sedans found more buyers in 1965. 4. Tapered taillight sections made the Wildcat look even bigger than its exterior dimensions suggested. "Wildcats come in three strengths," the advertisements promised: "wild (325 hp), wilder (340 hp), wildest (360 hp)." Standard Wildcat engine was a 401-cid/325-hp V-8. The optional 425-cid engine came in two flavors: 340 or 360 hp. 5. Wildcat dashboards were typical of the times, with colorful interiors. Buick's automatic transmission was standard, with a column-mounted lever. Production reached an all-time record in 1965, with nearly 99,000 Wildcats sent to Buick dealerships.

4

5

1

1. "Big and beautiful" might easily describe the 1965 Wildcat convertible, now that it had adopted the 126-inch wheelbase of the Buick Electra 225. Familiar Wildcat design cues were modified to mate with the redesigned, more rounded body. Convertibles were marketed in Deluxe and upscale Custom trim, priced at $3,502 and $3,727, respectively. 2. Bucket-style front seats flanked a long console, which contained the shift lever for the automatic transmission. Note the two big, round instrument clusters sitting low on the dashboard, and the immense (by today's standards) glovebox door. 3. Spare tires were full-size in 1965, taking up space in what would otherwise be an abundantly dimensioned trunk. 4. Wildcat engine choices started with the standard 401-cid V-8, but buyers could choose from a pair of 425s, cranking out as much as 360 hp. All but one of the Wildcat models topped the two-ton mark, but weights were actually similar to those of their smaller 1964 predecessors.

2

3

4

1

Top dog of the midsize Skylark lineup was the new Gran Sport, marketed in three body styles: coupe, hardtop coupe, and convertible. Veering away from Buick's past image, responding to the debut of Pontiac's GTO, the GS packed a 401-cid "Nailhead" V-8.

2

3

4

1. Best-selling Skylark Gran Sport model was the $2,751 two-door hardtop. More than 47,000 hardtops rolled off Buick's assembly line in 1965, versus 11,877 regular GS coupes and 10,456 convertibles. 2. A "Gran Sport" emblem on the C-pillar announced that this particular midsize Buick was a serious performance machine, joining the growing list of intermediate muscle cars. 3. Like other midsize models, the Skylark GS rode a 115-inch wheelbase, but oversize tires hit the pavement with greater passion. Dual exhaust pipes helped enhance the Gran Sport's performance image, though Buick's midsize GS never quite reached the same icon status as the Pontiac GTO. Note the elongated "portholes" on front fenders, still a Buick hallmark in 1965. 4. Dubbed the Wildcat 445 (and used in Buick's Wildcat series), the 401-cid V-8 beneath the hood of a Skylark Gran Sport sent its 325 energetic horses—and a 445 pound-feet torque wallop—to a Super Turbine 300 automatic transmission. Because of the Skylark's comparatively light weight, that was enough to send a GS to 60 mph in a brisk 7.4 seconds—an eminently respectable acceleration figure in 1965.

1

2

3

4

5

1, 2. Previously an offshoot of the Buick Special, which had been transformed from a compact into a midsize model in 1964, the Skylark became a fully separate series this year. The regular Skylark convertible sold in far fewer numbers than its Gran Sport counterpart, which had a big-block V-8 engine rather than a mild-mannered Fireball V-6 or a small V-8. Only 1,181 of the regular open Skylarks were produced. Convertibles were also offered in the less-expensive Special series. 3. A narrow center console separated the bucket-styled seats in a Skylark convertible, which was upholstered in vinyl—a familiar sight in automobiles of the mid Sixties. Note the wide speedometer in a businesslike instrument panel. Three-speed manual shift was standard, but Skylarks could have a four-speed or a two-speed Super Turbine 300 automatic transmission. 4. Skylarks had two engine choices: Buick's 225-cid V-6, rated at 155 hp, or a small-block 300-cid V-8 that yielded a minimum of 210 hp, boosted to 250 if equipped with a four-barrel carburetor. 5. The four-door sedan was one of five Skylark body styles, and the most popular non-Gran Sport model.

1

Now in its third season, the stylish Riviera personal-luxury coupe gained a fresh face for its final outing before a dramatic redesign. Considered the most desirable Riviera, the 1963-65 generation helped usher in a new way of thinking about plush personal transportation.

2

3

4

5

1-3. No longer exposed at the grille edges, Riviera headlights were now stacked vertically behind electrically operated "clamshell" doors in front fenders. Taillights were newly recessed into the back bumper, and dummy side scoops behind each door were deleted. The new Gran Sport option featured wood trim, as well as a limited-slip differential, quicker steering, and a firmer suspension with "Gyro-Poise" roll control. Special five-spoke wheels were available only on the GS edition. 4. Rivieras helped set the pace in interior luxury and style. Note the separately mounted tachometer and the long slanted console, reaching up to the dashboard. 5. A "Riviera Gran Sport" emblem ahead of the door denoted the presence of a 360-hp, 425-cid V-8, rather than the Riviera's standard 401-cid engine. Volume dipped to just 34,586 units.

CADILLAC

Tailfins, prominent since 1948, finally were planed down to create the 1965 Cadillac. Result: to many eyes, one of the best looking Cadillacs of the postwar era. Beneath the long and shapely body was a new, more-rigid box-section perimeter frame, helping to make the '65 model stronger and quieter.

1

2

3

1, 2. Part of Cadillac's lineup since 1949, the Coupe de Ville was one of four de Ville body styles—and the second most popular. A modified suspension improved the ride. New vertically stacked headlights permitted a wider grille. Elongated, squared-off rear fenders gave the impression of fins. Pillared four-door sedans returned for the first time since 1958, ousting the previous six-window hardtop sedans. Curved side glass was new this year. All Cadillacs had a 429-cid V-8, rated at 340 hp with new "sonically balanced" exhaust and driving a three-speed automatic transmission. 3. More than 19,000 Cadillac fans drove home a de Ville convertible in 1965, paying $5,639 for the privilege. 4. Standard Cadillacs rode a 129.5-inch wheelbase, but not the extra-posh Fleetwood Sixty Special four-door sedan, which mounted a 133-inch span. Output was impressive, at 18,100 units, for a $6,479 automobile. An Eldorado convertible commanded even more dollars.

4

CHEVROLET

Popularity of midsize models was growing fast in the mid Sixties. Chevrolet's new-for-'64 Chevelle occupied a substantial chunk of that market, competing primarily against Ford's Fairlane. It also served as the foundation for Chevrolet's first midsize musclecar, the Malibu Super Sport. A handful of fortunate folks got the new breed of SS in 1965, packing the new 396-cid big-block V-8.

1

2

3

4

1. Of the 101,577 Malibu SS models produced in 1965, a mere 201—including this red hardtop—were equipped with the Z16 option, which featured a 396-cid Turbo-Jet V-8 that cranked out 375 hp. For 1965, a lengthened hood sat above a vee'd grille. Available as a hardtop coupe or a convertible, Malibu SS models had flat-black grille accents, helping to establish a trend toward blacked-out front ends. 2. Dubbed the "porcupine" engine because of its valvetrain configuration, the 396 V-8 turned an already strong Malibu SS into a true screamer. The Z16 option added $1,501 to the basic $2,647 price of an SS hardtop. Could it travel? A 0-60 mph acceleration time of six seconds answers that question emphatically. 3. Malibu SS models displayed less chrome than other Chevelles. Any Chevelle powertrain was available in the SS series, with up to 350 hp available from the 327-cid V-8. Like its midsize mates, the Malibu SS got a mild facelift for 1965, with a lower profile and measuring a bit longer overall, on a 115-inch wheelbase. 4. During the 1965 model year, Malibu SS interiors switched from their initial corduroy pattern to textured vinyl front bucket seats.

1

An El Camino car/pickup had joined Chevrolet's stable for 1959, but went on hiatus after 1960. It returned for '64, at which time it switched from full-size to midsize, moving onto the Chevelle platform. For '65, the handy little pickup got a new face, which it shared with parent Chevelle.

2

1. Chevrolet launched the revived El Camino during the middle of the 1964 model year, after a three-season hiatus. Decades later, as the 21st century dawned, automakers were promoting "crossover" vehicles that combined the merits of a truck and a passenger car—essentially, the utility of a truck mixed with the comforts, conveniences, and ride/handling qualities of a regular automobile. Chevrolet and Ford both seem to have gotten the idea far earlier, when introducing their hybrid car/pickups in the late 1950s. Ford called its version the Ranchero, also moving from its original full-size platform to a midsize chassis in the Sixties. 2. Viewed from the front, an El Camino looked little different from the midsize Chevelle passenger car on which it was based. Powertrains and trim levels were also shared between the two. Parking lights were inset into a slotted front bumper, below a horizontally split grille. 3. El Caminos with bucket seats and floor-shifted four-speed manual transmissions could be ordered, but this interior has a standard bench and a three-speed gearshift on the steering column. Most of the accessories offered on Chevelles also could be installed in El Caminos.

3

Criticism of the first-generation Corvair's handling produced a notable suspension change for 1965, along with a freshly rounded design for the innovative compact. Critics declared the new shape a stunner.

1

2

3

4

1, 2. Sleeker and more rounded than its 1961-64 predecessors, a Corvair Monza two-door hardtop sold for $2,347. This one has the 110-hp engine option. Minimal trim helped give the impression of a European design. Pillared coupes and sedans were gone, replaced by hardtop body styles. The 1965 lineup included a Corvair 500, midrange Monza, and a new top-line Corsa. The Corsa replaced the Monza Spyder, and had a standard four-carb 140-hp engine. It could be fitted with a turbocharger, which boosted horsepower to a stout 180. 3. Monza convertible production totaled 26,466 units—quite a score for a ragtop in 1965. Soft-topped Corsas added 8,353 to the Corvair total, which passed the 200,000 mark. 4. Marketers considered keeping the Monza Spyder name, but turned instead to Corsa. The new, fully independent rear suspension eliminated allegations of tricky handling. Though similar to the suspension used in Corvettes, it used coil springs rather than a transverse leaf.

Conservative in look and tone, the Chevy II provided sensible transportation for countless families since its debut for 1962. With a hotter V-8 under its hood, however, this seemingly square compact adopted quite a potent personality.

1

2

1. With a modest six-cylinder engine, the Chevy II 100 two-door sedan went for just $2,077. Sedans sported a new, almost formal roofline, along with fresh front/rear styling. 2. In base 100 trim, a radio would cost extra, but this Texas sedan is air conditioned. Note the column shift and bench seat. 3. Despite its practical virtues, the Chevy II was the only General Motors car to post a sales decline in 1965. 4. A 283-cid V-8 powers this Chevy II two-door hardtop. At midyear, a 220-hp version of the 283 joined the options list, identified by dual exhaust pipes. For truly serious muscle, a new 327-cid V-8 cranked out 250 horses in regular trim, or even a whopping 300—quite an imposing figure for such a light vehicle.

3

4

1

Right in the middle of the Sting Ray generation, Chevrolet introduced a big-block V-8 option for its Corvette sports car. "Fuelies" were in their final season, and new standard all-disc brakes brought the hot two-seater to a quick halt.

2

3

4

1, 2. A side-mounted exhaust system clearly conveys the impression of brute force on this Corvette Sting Ray convertible, which carries the optional fuel-injected 327-cid V-8, sending 375 hp to a four-speed manual gearbox. A smoothed-down hood eliminated the former sculpted shape, and the previous dummy front-fender slots were transformed into functional vents. 3. Corvette drivers enjoyed more supportive seats in 1965, and instruments were revised a bit. Integrated armrests were new. Corvette production consisted of 8,186 coupes and 15,376 convertibles. Soft top Corvettes sold for $4,106, while the closed coupes commanded $4,321. 4. A quick glance identifies this V-8 as the fuel-injected version, which would be dropped from the option list after 1965. Carbureted engines started at a milder 250 hp, but other choices stretched the limit to 365 hp. Introduced in 1953, Chevrolet's two-seater was the only serious sports car produced by an American automaker at this time.

1

1. Who wouldn't be willing—more likely, eager—to pay an extra $293 for the new Mark IV "porcupine" V-8 engine, displacing 396 cubic inches and whipping up no fewer than 425 frenzied horses? Alluring as it sounds today, only 2,157 of the big-block options were sold in 1965, with four-barrel carburetion and an 11:1 compression ratio, as well as a double-snorkel air cleaner and a bigger radiator than usual. The Turbo-Jet 396 engine package also included a super-duty clutch, stiffer front springs and antisway bar, and a special rear antisway bar. An aggressively shaped hood bulge helped identify the presence of the hottest engine, and side-mounted exhaust pipes were also available. 2. A side profile view shows off the Corvette coupe's heavily slanted, one-piece back glass. Even in its tamer forms, of course, the Corvette delivered sensational performance. 3. Rocker panel trim was revised for 1965. This was Corvette's first year with standard four-wheel disc brakes.

2

3

1

Full-size Chevrolet bodies grew in size for 1965, gaining rounded sides and curved window glass. Bel Air continued as the midrange series, between the "entry-level" Biscayne and the costlier Impala—including the Super Sport offshoot that had launched in 1961. Halfway through the season, Chevrolet's 396-cid V-8 became available.

2

1. A 327-cid V-8 sits under the hood of this Impala SS (Super Sport) convertible, which was also available with the standard 230-cid six-cylinder engine—though not many were so equipped. Super Sports looked similar to regular Impalas, but they lacked the latter's rocker sill and lower fender trim. Bodysides displayed "Super Sport" identification. 2. In keeping with sporty-car expectations, Impala SS interiors featured bucket seats. A tachometer added to the Super Sport driving experience. 3. Block letters within the grille spelled out "Impala SS." New triple-blade SS wheel covers quickly became popular. This car carries nonfactory wide-whitewall tires. 4. A trio of triple round taillights sat at each side of the Impala's rear end.

4

3

1

2

1, 2. What might be lurking beneath the hood of this Impala SS two-door hardtop? Nothing less than the legendary 409-cid V-8, delivering its 340 hp to a floor-shifted four-speed manual gearbox. A 400-hp version was also listed. Before long, the 409 would be extinct, ousted by the new 396-cid V-8 that arrived during the 1965 model year. The new engine came in modest 325-hp form, or set up to unleash an astounding 425 horses.
3. Introduced as a midseason option package for the Impala four-door hardtop, the Caprice would become a separate model for 1966. Essentially an Impala with fancier upholstery and trim, the Caprice was Chevrolet's response to the Ford LTD.

3

1

Full-size Oldsmobiles wore new Fisher C-bodies, with a reshaped roofline and bigger trunk. The curvy sheetmetal was shared with Cadillac, and with the Buick Electra 225. Luxury-minded families could pick a Ninety-Eight sedan, but the sportier Starfire promised a little more flair.

2

3

4

1. Well over 12,000 shoppers got a Ninety-Eight two-door hardtop in 1965. Serving to identify the most posh Oldsmobile product, Ninety-Eight was one of the older model names still in existence, dating to 1941. Even though the body was completely new, Oldsmobile retained the familiar "dumbbell" grille shape from previous models. The Ninety-Eight's wheelbase measured 126 inches. 2. A broad bench seat with fold-down armrest greeted the driver, who controlled the automatic transmission with a conventional column-mounted gear selector. Oldsmobile's top V-8 engine grew to 425 cid, producing 360 hp when installed in a Ninety-Eight but only 310 in a Delta 88 or Dynamic 88, which rode a 3-inch shorter wheelbase. 3. Oldsmobile's Starfire came in two body styles, on a 123-inch wheelbase. More than 13,000 hardtop coupes were produced. A T-stick on the console, between the bucket seats, operated the Turbo Hydra-Matic transmission.
4. Considering their abundant dimensions, Starfires handled quite capably. Manual gearboxes were making their way into sporty renditions of America's big cars, and a floor-shifted four-speed was available in a Starfire. Convertibles started at $4,778, versus $4,138 for the Starfire hardtop, and volume totaled a modest 2,236 units.

Like other automakers in 1965, Oldsmobile focused strongly on its midsize models—the everyday F-85 and the tantalizing Cutlass, which attracted a more enthusiastic breed of driver. Hottest Cutlass of all was the 4-4-2, now in its second season.

1

2

3

1. Riding a 115-inch wheelbase, Cutlass models came in three body styles, including the $2,983 convertible, which sold in fewer numbers than the sport coupe or two-door hardtop. Even so, production of 12,628 soft tops was an impressive showing. 2. Cutlass interiors looked quite conventional for their time, with a column-mounted shifter for the automatic transmission and a pair of bucket seats up front. Note the horizontal-type speedometer, used in many 1965 automobiles. 3. Standard Cutlass engine was a 330-cid V-8, which developed 315 hp, identified by the "Ultra-High Compression" designation atop the air cleaner. In those days of readily available, low-priced gasoline, few seemed concerned about the need for premium fuel. Cutlass buyers also had a big-block choice, in the form of a 400-cid/320-hp V-8. 4. Cutlass was the only midsize convertible, but ragtops were available in the larger Jetstar 88, Dynamic 88, Starfire, and Ninety-Eight series.

4

1

2

3

4

5

1. Younger drivers gravitated toward Cutlass hardtops with the 4-4-2 package, which added only about $156 to the basic price. On an F-85, the option cost $190. Added midseason 1964, it was available on any F-85/Cutlass coupe or convertible. Note the special lower-body trim, redline tires, and wire wheelcovers. 2. Initially, the 4-4-2 designation stood for a four-speed manual transmission, four-barrel carburetor, and dual exhaust. The performance-packed option was actually a spinoff of the Cutlass/F-85 police package. 3. In 1964, the 4-4-2 option had included a 330-cid/310-hp V-8. Oldsmobile upped the ante for 1965, installing a 400-cid V-8 that made 345 hp and packed a 440 pound-feet torque blast. A 4-4-2 Olds could reach 60 mph in 7.5 seconds. 4. Heavy-duty shocks, springs, rear axle, driveshaft, wheels, and other components were part of the modestly-priced 4-4-2 package, adding to its attractiveness among enthusiastic drivers who might otherwise lean toward Pontiac's GTO. 5. Bucket seats flanked a long console in the Cutlass 4-4-2, which could have a heavy-duty three-speed stick, a close-ratio four-speed, or Jetaway 400 automatic. Notice the T-selector gearshift in this example.

1

Not many Sixties automobiles even approach the panache of Pontiac's GTO—especially in its early form. Part of the Tempest LeMans series, the GTO was now in its second season, about to see sales double to more than 75,000 units.

2

3

4

1. Style, sport, and power marked the GTO convertible, which sold for $3,057 in 1965. Standard GTO engine was a 389-cid V-8, increased to 335 hp this year. Selecting the Tri-Power option, with triple carburetion, raised the stakes to 360 hp. That was sufficient to yield 0-60 mph acceleration figures in the low six-second neighborhood. 2. All LeMans models, including the GTO, were facelifted with crisper lines, taillights positioned in a ribbed panel across the deck, and new vertical headlights. 3. A ball-type knob for the four-speed floor shifter added to the GTO's allure. Note the narrow-rim, three-spoke steering wheel. GTO buyers could pick from a wide range of performance add-ons, including metallic brake linings and a limited-slip differential. 4. This GTO insignia soon came to signify solid American performance, setting the stage for the muscle-car era. Immortalized in song and story, the GTO remains one of the most sought-after automobiles of its generation.

1

Bonnevilles looked even bigger than they were, at a time when full-size automobiles were still a major force in motoring. Restyled for 1965, Bonnevilles and Star Chiefs bulged and blossomed, stretching to greater lengths. Buyers responded by driving home 165,000 biggies.

2

3

4

1. Bonneville was the largest of five convertibles in Pontiac's full-size lineup, with a $3,594 sticker price and production of 21,050 units—the top-selling soft top model of 1965. Full-size Pontiacs featured fender skirts. Tires had narrow whitewalls, and the dual exhaust pipes suggest an abundance of power beneath the hood. 2. Three occupants enjoyed elbow room on the front bench seat of a Bonneville. Woodgrain trim complemented the instrument panel, with its horizontal speedometer and trio of round gauges in the center. 3. Standard engine in the Bonneville was a relatively mild-mannered 389-cid V-8, but the optional 421-cid V-8 could unleash as much as 376 hp. 4. Stacked quad headlights and a prominent split grille made the Bonneville easy to spot at a glance. Bonnevilles and Star Chiefs rode a 124-inch wheelbase.

1

2

3

4

1, 2. Pontiac had launched the Bonneville nameplate in 1957, strictly as a top-of-the-line convertible, then increased its scope gradually into a full selection of body styles. Which Bonneville model sold the strongest in 1965? The four-door pillarless hardtop, with 62,480 examples rolling off the assembly line. Full-size Pontiacs grew significantly bulkier in size this year, but weights did not increase correspondingly. Road-testers at *Motor Trend* magazine managed to accelerate a Bonneville to 60 mph in 9.1 seconds—respectable time for a full-size model. Flashy trim, as on the bright lower-body panels, still attracted customer dollars—especially as they moved up the General Motors status scale from Chevrolet to Cadillac, making stops at Buick, Olds, or Pontiac.

3, 4. Of the four Bonneville body styles, the two-door Sport hardtop proved to be second in popularity, with 44,030 produced and a $3,357 sticker price. All hardtops gained a semifastback roof profile. Two-door Pontiacs could have bucket seats for an extra $116. The Bonneville lineup also included a Safari station wagon, while full-size Star Chiefs came only in four-door sedan and hardtop sedan form, commanding more moderate prices.

1

Pontiac set the pace for personal-luxury transportation with its almost full-size Grand Prix coupe and the similarly dimensioned Catalina—the latter available with appealing 2+2 styling. Midsize models were gaining strength, though, causing Grand Prix sales to begin a distressing slump.

2

3

4

1. Introduced in 1964, the Catalina 2+2 hardtop coupe was actually a $419 option package for the two-door hardtop ($397 for the convertible), identified by fender louvers and pinstriping, plus special hood/deck badging. 2. Breathing through a trio of carburetors, the Catalina 2+2's optional Tri-Power 421-cid V-8 stirred up 376 horses. All 2+2 models had a 421-cid V-8, though the 1964 models made do with 389 cubic inches. The 2+2 package included a three-speed Hurst floor shift (four-speed optional), heavy-duty shocks and springs, and a performance axle. 3, 4. Like its full-size mates, the Grand Prix hardtop coupe got a bigger body for 1965, with flared rear quarters, but it retained the prior roofline and concave back window. Underneath, a full perimeter frame replaced the previous X-member configuration, providing greater side-impact protection. A 389-cid V-8 engine was standard, but this example holds the optional 421 V-8. Sales dipped to 57,881 units, but despite competition from midsizes, the $3,498 Grand Prix continued to serve as a guidepost for the personal-luxury coupe segment.

1965
1965
1965

STUDEBAKER

Though it was taking great pains to appear healthy, Studebaker was terminally ill in 1965, and car buyers knew it. Marketed under the banner, "The Common-Sense Cars," Studebaker pruned the once diverse lineup to a precious few models. Gone were Hawk and Avanti (though the latter would later experience a rebirth). Gone too was the Lark name. What remained were Commander two- and four-door sedans and a four-door station wagon, as well as a Cruiser four-door sedan. Rounding out the offerings were the Daytona Sport two-door sedan and Daytona Wagonaire. Prices ranged from a base of $2,125 for a Commander two-door to $3,505 for the Wagonaire.

The 1965 models were essentially the same as the '64 models. Studebaker tried to put a positive spin on the absence of newness in the lineup, noting that a lack of change would make for a lack of visual obsolescence. "Studebaker's beautiful modern style doesn't need yearly styling changes" a '65 sales brochure explained, "The money saved is passed on to you, in added comfort and quality, and in continuing engineering improvements." Few buyers accepted the premise, their attention distracted by the company's shaky financial condition.

The South Bend plant had been shuttered by this time and all cars were produced in Hamilton, Ontario, Canada. All Studebaker models were powered by McKinnon engines—built to Chevy design specifications by GM's Canadian facilities. Studebaker's engine offerings numbered just two for '65. The Skybolt six measured 194-cid and produced 120-hp. The Thunderbolt 283-cid V-8 was rated at 195-hp. Studebaker's sales literature trumpeted the virtues of the "husky" new Thunderbolt motor thusly: "Alive with power, alert to your slightest whim, but so very gentle with fuel." On the other hand, the Skybolt six was, "Smooth, responsive, dependable and economical…gives you power to spare on either in-city or cross-country driving."

Without the capital to design new product, there was little in the way of innovation for Studebaker in '65. At midyear, a transistorized ignition became standard on the Daytona Sport sedan and optional elsewhere in the lineup. Lack of money had also kept the company from fixing some known problems, like the sliding roof on the Wagonaires. Though ahead of its time in versatility, the open-roof wagons were notorious leakers—and thus precocious rusters.

Even as the company was dying, part of Studebaker's past was in the process of being reborn. A pair of former Studebaker dealership partners—Leo Newman and Nate Altman—teamed up to purchase the tooling, parts, and rights necessary to continue building Avantis. Taking on a small group of ex South Bend employees, they began producing an extremely limited run of Avanti IIs. Newman, Altman, and company bought a portion of the now dormant Studebaker factory and set to work, with a goal of building 300 Avanti IIs per year.

Fiberglass body panels were provided by the Molded Fiber Glass Body Company. Engines were courtesy of Chevrolet—specifically, a Corvette 327 V-8—backed by either automatic or a Borg-Warner four-speed manual transmission.

On the outside, one was hard pressed to tell the sequels from the originals. The only giveaway was that the new versions sat level, as opposed to the slight rake of the older models. Inside, it was a different story. One of the benefits of limited as opposed to mass production was that customers could have their car's interior tailored just about any way they pleased. Virtually any material available could be sewn into the cabin of an Avanti II. Custom exterior colors were offered too, providing latter day enthusiasts with more clues as to whether you were viewing a first series car or one of its successors. A wide range of options helped buyers further customize their Avanti.

First-generation Avantis could be fitted out as very serious high-performance cars. With the Avanti IIs the accent was more on luxury—four-place touring cars of considerable style. Also considerable, however, was their rarity; despite their stated goal of 300 cars, the actual number of '65 Avanti IIs produced was just 21.

While Avanti would go on to live not just one but several afterlives, its parent was not so lucky. In model year 1965, the company sold 19,435 cars, placing it 13th industrywide, sandwiched between low-production luxury marques Lincoln (12th) and Imperial (14th). Studebaker actually showed a profit on vehicle production for the year. Sadly, the positive cash flow was not nearly enough to stem the tide of corporate red ink. The company would soldier on for one more year before ceasing production.

1

Studebaker returned for 1965 with a thinned-out lineup, missing some high-profile players like the Hawk and the Avanti. 1. The Cruiser Sedan added a six-cylinder model for '65, complementing the existing V-8 models. Cruisin' with a six cost $2,470, while the V-8 version stickered for $2,610—seven dollars more than a '64 and the highest price for any nonwagon model. 2. Riding a 113-inch wheelbase, the Cruiser was visually almost the same as the '64. Though due to dwindling design funds, Studebaker tried to put a positive spin on the lack of freshening. "The elimination of yearly styling changes protects the investment in your new Studebaker," the sales brochure touted, "and will keep your new car looking new year after year." 3, 4. Studebaker invited buyers to step inside and get comfortable in the Cruiser's roomy, six-passenger interior, saying, "You can stretch your legs out, your hat doesn't bump the roof...." 5. Daytona model line for '65 was trimmed by two. Gone were the convertible and hardtop, remaining were the station wagon and two-door Sport Sedan (shown), which was priced at $2,565. 6. Power for all V-8 models was provided by the 283-cid/195-hp Thunderbolt V-8. The Chevy designed engines were built in Canada by McKinnon.

2

3

4

5

6

1965 1965 1965

IMPORTS

It can be safely said that the best-selling imports in 1965 were the Beatles, and the Beetles. The former—a quartet of shaggy-haired young men from Liverpool—were in the process of taking the country by storm. The latter—distinctly round, two-door sedans from Germany—were getting Americans used to the idea of economy cars.

American consciousness about imported cars in the mid Sixties was still rather limited. To the extent that we thought about imports at all in 1965, most people considered them to be in one of two camps: sports cars or small economy cars. Some of the foreign firms who would sell huge volumes on these shores in the Seventies were just in the process of establishing a beachhead, or hadn't even been seen yet.

The prototypical subcompact of the era was the VW Beetle. Volkswagen had landed their first imports in the states in 1950. What followed was decades of cars that looked more alike than different. Mechanical and cosmetic improvements appeared periodically—most found under the skin. For 1965, upgrades arrived on the exterior as well as under the skin. The Beetle gained 15 percent more glass area. The engine compartment cover was now accessed by means of a pushbutton as opposed to a t-handle. Longer windshield wipers were fitted and powered by a bigger motor.

Inside, front seats were recontoured and slimmed down, while rear seats showed newfound dexterity; they now folded virtually flat, allowing use of the space for stowing parcels. Heater controls were modified to increase air volume. Thermostatic controls of vents now allowed air to flow as soon as the engine was turned on. (As VW owners would attest, whether the engine would ever get warm enough to throw heat was a separate question!)

The flat-four engine that had been bumped up to a robust 40 hp in 1961 remained unchanged for '65. The bug would scuttle from 0-60 in a leisurely 22 seconds, but it returned a frugal 28-32 mpg. Two-door sedan, sunroof sedan, and convertible models were offered, starting at $1,563.

The sportier Karmann Ghia enjoyed the same upgrades as brother beetle. The two-door coupe sold for $2,250, while the convertible stickered for $2,445. The Transporter (aka the Microbus) was largely a holdover from '64, except that the 1500cc engine was now standard equipment.

Just two VWs made the trek across the pond to America in 1949, their first year of availability here. But 16 years later, it was a different story: 371,222 VW's were sold stateside in 1965.

Among the other brands that ultimately become small-car stars, Japanese names predominate. Honda was not yet on the American scene in '65. The first 600 series sedans didn't arrive on the West Coast until 1969. By then, Toyota was already in residence, and sold 130,044 vehicles. But in '65, just 6,404 Toyotas took on American citizenship. Known then as Toyopets, passenger-car offerings were named Tiara and Crown. Both models were offered as four-door sedans and the latter was also available as a station wagon.

Datsun's 1965 lineup was well-rounded. It included a subcompact sedan known as the 410, a deluxe sedan called the Cedric, a sporty roadster, compact pickup truck, and a 4×4. A midmodel year change brought an upgrade to the little roadster: the Fairlady 1500 was superseded by the Sports 1600. Upgrades between the old and new sports cars were substantial. The 97-cid engine now made 96 hp and 103 pound-feet of torque, and the car topped out at 100 mph. Stopping was improved, too (front disc brakes became standard), and shifting was a breeze thanks to an all-synchro gearbox and improved clutch.

The Datsun 1600 had a decidedly British look to it. The Brits, for their part, were busy building what would become known as sports-car classics. MG's most notable entry in this category was the MGB. Succeeding the A series for 1963, '65 Bs benefited from a new oil cooler, rear oil seal, and five-bearing crankshaft. MGBs from this era were cleanly styled and beautifully balanced sports cars.

Triumph's U.S. lineup consisted of the Spitfire and TR4A. The latter was new for the model year. While outwardly appearing much the same as the TR4 that had preceded it, the "A" version offered improvements on two fronts. First, the four-cylinder engine was massaged for an additional 4 hp to 104, and top speed approached 110 mph. More significant were chassis changes. Independent rear suspension replaced the live-axle setup, bringing vast improvements in handling and ride quality. A total of 20,347 Triumphs were sold stateside for the year.

Jaguar's '65 lineup included the sporting E-Type, graceful Mk II, and the elegant Mk X. The Jaguar straight six was bored out to 4.2 liters for '65 and placed in E-Types and the Mk X. Horsepower ratings remained the same 265 as before, but torque improved to 283 pound-feet. It was coupled to a new all-synchro four-speed gearbox in the E-Type.

Mercedes fielded five series for '65: 190, 220, 300SE, 230SL, and the 600s. Elsewhere amongst German manufacturers, U.S. Porschefiles witnessed the birth of a legend with the introduction of the 911 series for 1965. Though showing an obvious family resemblance to the 356 models, the 911 was of sleeker styling, with the rounded lines of the 356 eschewed for a flatter, sharper look. The 911 kept the 2+2 configuration of its predecessors, and stretched it about a half-foot longer. The horizontally-opposed, flat six engine was rated at 148 hp and coupled to either a four- or five-speed transaxle. Brakes were discs all around. The 911 had a look-alike sibling as well—a four-cylinder version designated the 912. Additionally, the 356s were still being sold alongside the models that would replace them by year's end.

Opel offered a trio of little cars in the American market. Kadett models were introduced in two-door coupe, sedan, and station wagon body styles. Some 17,378 Opel cars were imported in '65.

Saab's 96 and 95 and Monte Carlo 850 models were treated to new styling, growing almost six inches in length and featuring a longer, flatter front clip. The two-cycle, three-cylinder engines got a nominal boost in horsepower—96 and 95 models gained 2 hp to 44; Monte Carlos got 3 hp to 60. A total of 5,462 Saab models were sold stateside.

The other Swedish manufacturer, Volvo, had a U.S. contingent of five models derived from three series. The oldest design offered was the 544, a sedan that could trace its lineage back to the WWII era. The venerable two-door was in its final official year in '65, though some leftovers would be sold as '66s. Linemates to the 544 were the 122S series two- and four-door sedans and four-door wagons. The other entry was the 1800S—a sporty two-door coupe with a sticker price of $3,920.

Fiat's imports included a price-leading two-door 600 series sedan ($1,262), four-door sedans and station wagons from the 1100 series, and the sleek little Spider convertible. Just under 8,200 '65 Fiats were sold in the U.S.

In 1965, a year in which Chevrolet alone sold over 2.3 million vehicles, few imports were as yet raising a blip on the American radar screen. Most dramatic is the almost complete absence of Japanese manufacturers—Chevy sold more '65 Corvair Monza convertibles than all the combined models of all the Japanese automakers taken together in the same year. Ten years hence, it would be quite a different story.

1

2

3

4

1. Datsun's Fairlady 1500 came relatively well-equipped, with standard radio, heater, tonneau cover, crank-up windows, and four-speed transmission. Partway through the '65 model year, it was replaced by the 1600, which included such upgrades as a 96-hp motor, front disc brakes, and an all-synchro gearbox. 2. The Ferrari 275 GTB/6C featured fully-independent suspension and a 3.3-litre V-12 engine. Buyers of Series I, "short nose" GTB's like this one could choose from three or six Weber carburetors, and steel/aluminum or all-aluminum bodywork. Borrani wire wheels were optional as well. 3. The Sunbeam Tiger was hotter than its look-alike linemate, the Alpine. The difference was the 260-cid/164-hp Ford V-8 that propelled the Tiger. This "civilized Cobra" couldn't match the celebrated snake for performance, but offered far more refinement for less money. 4. A larger, 4.2-litre engine was new to Jaguar's E-Type for 1965. More torque and an all-synchro gearbox made the new E-Type more fun to drive, while better binders made it easier to stop. 5. The Lamborghini 350 GT harbored a 280-hp V-12, crowned by six Weber carbs.

5

1

2

1. Morgan's +4 roadsters soldiered on for '65 as distinctly retro-looking sports cars, with styling cues dating to prewar times. +4 bodywork was done in-house, with virtually everything else farmed out. 2. One classy little variant on the traditional Morgan theme was the +4+. Riding on a +4 chassis, these fiberglass-bodied, fixed-roof coupes were powered by Triumph TR4 engines and were notable for their distinctive styling. With laid-back grillwork and an upright, bell-shaped top, the +4+ was rarely seen, then or now; just 26 were built between 1963-66. 3. After a run of some 15 years, Porsche's 356 series was retired in September 1965. This '65 Cabriolet has the 88-hp, 1600-cc engine. 4. Inside shot shows the businesslike accommodations of a 356C Coupe. 5. Although growing dated by this time, the venerable 356 design was nonetheless still quite attractive. In their last year of production, 356 models were sold alongside new family members designated the 912 and the 911. The latter would carry the company flag forward into the next century.

3

4

5

1. Early in model year 1965, Triumph rolled out the Mark 2 series of its Spitfires. Mark 2 cars gained four more hp than their predecessors, to 67. Also new were a vinyl-covered dashboard instead of painted metal, improved seat material, and carpeting in place of the former rubber floormats. Base price was $2,199. A total of 9,097 '65 Spitfires were sold stateside. 2. Spitfire's big brother was the TR4, which for 1965 gave way to the TR4A. Revisions in the new model were mostly found under the skin. The standard engine was now rated at 104 hp, but more important were its chassis upgrades. A stiffer platform with independent rear suspension replaced the live-axle setup. 3. The TVR Griffith was the result of a marriage between an American engine and a British body and chassis. Essentially a TVR Grantura with 289 Ford V-8 added, the Griffith was originally an export-only model, becoming available in Great Britain as well as America for 1965. 4. An Italian-designed body with German underpinnings, the Karmann Ghia was sold alongside the Volkswagen sedan from 1956 to 1974. 5. The most popular 1965 import by far was the Volkswagen Beetle, which for that year was almost identical to the '66 shown here. Three versions of the bug were offered for '65: the $1,563 two-door sedan, a sunroof sedan for an additional $100, and a convertible for $2,053. On September 15, 1965, the company built its 10,000,000th Volkswagen. 6. Late in 1964, production of Volvo's sporty looking P1800 coupe switched from England to Sweden. At the same time, the 1800 models were designated 1800S and got minor cosmetic changes. Never a big seller, the 1800 series cars nonetheless helped change the way some people thought about safe and staid Volvo.

1

2

3

4

5

6

1965
1965
1965

MISCELLANEOUS

As had been the case for decades before, the Big Three cast a large shadow over the automotive landscape during the Sixties. But a handful of tiny independent manufacturers continued to survive—thrive in some cases—by serving unique specialty niches that large automakers didn't take note of or considered too small to be profitable.

Unlike the major makes, these mini manufacturers were often inextricably tied to the individuals that ran them—typically the company's founder, president, and chief engineer. As a result, they offer a flavorful counterpoint to the faceless entities that were the larger automakers of the period.

Morris Markin came to America at the start of WWI, and in the early Twenties formed what would become the Checker Cab Manufacturing Company. For decades, the bread-and-butter of Markin's company was building taxicabs. But in 1959, Checker began to more aggressively promote its line of consumer sedans and wagons, in response to a declining cab market.

The '65 Checker consumer lineup continued the A12 design, introduced for '63. Available models for '65 were the Marathon four-door sedan and station wagon, Town Custom limousine, and six- and eight-door Aerobus station wagons. The A12 was just a few years into its life at this time, but it would be a long legacy indeed; this would prove to be the last of the big Checker designs, and it stayed in production into the Eighties.

John Fitch made a name for himself in the early Fifties racing in such noteworthy machines as the Mercedes 300SL and the Cunningham C4. But by 1962, he was concentrating much of his effort under the hood, heating up Chevy's Corvair into his own brand of GT car, which he called the Fitch Sprint.

For 1965, Fitch applied his modifications to the second-generation Corvair that was making its debut. He developed a line of some 40 different items, ranging from high-performance suspension pieces, to amenities such as a wooden shift knob. The parts could be installed by the owner, or, for a small premium, his company would handle the job at its facility in Falls Village, Connecticut.

Automotive stylist Virgil Exner is probably best remembered as the creator of Chrysler's late-Fifties "Forward Look" designs. But by the early Sixties, he had left Chrysler to set up his own freelance automotive design studio with his son Virgil, Jr.

The senior Exner had long been known for his love of Classic-era styling cues. Thus, his new studio was a natural pick when in 1963 *Esquire* magazine decided to run a series of automotive renderings that speculated what four extinct famous car makes might look like in the Sixties.

The Exners came up with neo-classic interpretations of Packard, Stutz, Duesenberg, and Mercer. At about this time, the Copper Development Association was seeking ways to showcase new uses for copper alloys, and felt Exner's Mercer would be an excellent means of doing so. In 1965, the organization commissioned the construction of one operational full-size car, and provided the various alloys that went into its trim.

Dale Orcutt and Claude Dry met and became friends as Civil Air Patrol pilots during WWII.

Fueled by their shared enthusiasm for tinkering, they formed Midget Motors after the war.

Their main product, the King Midget, was introduced in 1946. It began as a single-seater, styled like sort of an overgrown, quarter midget race car. By the early Fifties, it had evolved into a Jeepster-esque two-seater. Small improvements were incorporated into the rather simple, homespun looking cars, but the basic design remained essentially unchanged after 1957. Thus, the 1965 King Midget was virtually indistinguishable from those of the late Fifties.

Jeep wasn't the small-time operation many independents of the Sixties were, but the company successfully employed a similar niche marketing strategy. Significant rivals such as Ford Bronco and Chevrolet Blazer hadn't arrived yet, which allowed Jeep to work the small but steadily growing 4×4 market with little competitive pressure.

The CJ had always been Jeep's primary product and was still, by far, its most popular. For '65 it continued in its CJ-5 design first introduced for 1955. Alongside that was offered the long-wheelbase CJ-6 version. Rounding out the line was the Gladiator pickup and the Wagoneer station wagon on which it was based.

Perhaps the best known of the small independent manufacturers was the creation of illustrious Texan, Carroll Shelby. This brash, colorful figure first rose to fame as a successful race car driver in the Fifties. Shelby's career behind the wheel ended abruptly in 1960 when he was diagnosed with a heart condition. However, his retirement merely gave him more time to pursue his dream of building a relatively low-priced American sports car that was capable of beating the world's best.

Shelby put his plan into action in late 1961, when he conceived a plan to fit England's AC Ace sports car with an American V-8. Among major automakers, Ford Motor Company proved the most receptive to the concept, and provided its new 260-cid (later 289-cid) V-8.

The resulting Cobra design quickly proved competitive on the track, chalking up prestigious victories in the '63 and '64 seasons. But 1965 was the true pinnacle of the car's career. Shelby's team, consisting primarily of Cobra Daytona coupes, won the 1965 FIA World Manufacturer's Championship, beating nemesis Ferrari. Adding further luster to that year was the introduction of the 427 Cobra, arguably the most fearsome iteration of Shelby's little sports car.

As the big-engine Cobra was making its debut, Shelby was embarking on another equally significant collaboration. Ford's Mustang had proven an immediate success, but some within the division felt the little ponycar needed more of a performance image than could be afforded by its top V-8, the 271-hp 289. Thus, Ford asked Shelby to build a high-performance street version of the car and an all-out, race-ready variant.

The street Shelby Mustang, called G.T. 350, packed a hotter version of the 289 "HiPo" V-8, along with a host of other performance equipment. The "R" version of the G.T. 350 was a true competition-ready race car as delivered, with an even more potent 289 and a host of racing equipment.

From the homespun simplicity of the King Midget, to the artsy coachbuilt flavor of the Mercer Cobra, the products of America's tiny independents were a varied lot. Some were in the twilight of short careers in 1965, while others were in the midst of a long evolution that continues today. Whatever the case, the unique personalities of these specialized vehicles provide an enjoyable contrast to the general-market cars that surrounded them.

1

1, 2. The Checker Marathon was available in four-door sedan, or station wagon, shown here. For years, Checkers had been powered by Continental inline six-cylinder engines. Continental dropped the contract after 1964, so, from the '65 model year on, Checker turned to Chevrolet as its primary engine supplier. Available engines in '65 Checkers were a 230-cid/140-hp inline six, or a 283-cid/195-hp small-block V-8. 3. For users that required even more room than the cavernous Marathon interior could provide, Checker offered the Aerobus in nine-passenger six-door form (shown), or a 12-passenger eight-door. Built on a 152.5- or 189-inch wheelbase, the "bus" part of its name was certainly appropriate. 4. The '65 Marathon's interior, while certainly not taxicab austere, looked like what it was—a spruced up Fifties design. Owners didn't seem to care, appreciating instead the generous room and robust construction of the big cars.

2

3

4

1

1. John Fitch first began offering his modified Corvairs, called Fitch Sprints, for 1962. The '65 edition was based on the Corsa version of the redesigned second-generation Corvair. Visible on this Sprint is the most noticeable Fitch item, the "Sprint Fastback 904 Ventop." This $102 add-on attached to the roof, giving the car (from some angles) the appearance of a fastback. 2. Fitch also offered a number of interior amenities for his Corvairs, including this wood-rim, aluminum-spoke steering wheel and a shift knob made of "rich Brazilian Rosewood." 3. Central to the 1965 Sprint package was the GT suspension option, which cost $56 installed. It consisted of progressive-rate, rubber auxiliary springs for all four wheels and adjustable Gabriel rear shock absorbers. Also, the front suspension was reset to four degrees positive caster and a quarter degree positive camber. Rear camber was set to one and a half degrees negative. Complementing the GT package were several options for the steering system. Shorter steering arms quickened the ratio from 23:1 to a more sporting 15:1. Also available was a Delco steering damper borrowed from the Corvette Sting Ray. Underhood, Sprints had an additional 15 hp over the stock Corvair Corsa's 140, achieved with minor modifications that included a slightly altered crankcase breather, three additional degrees of ignition-timing advance, and four small air filters that replaced the single, centrally mounted stock unit. Visible up front are two yellow-tinted, Lucas "Flamethrower" driving lights, available from Fitch for $9.95 each.

2

3

1

1, 2. Virgil Exner first penned his neo-classic Mercer design for *Esquire* magazine. To showcase new uses for Copper, the Copper Development Association later commissioned this fully-operable one-off version, called the Mercer Cobra. It sported copper trim made from 11 different alloys, but the body itself was conventional steel, built by coachbuilder Sibona-Basano in Torino, Italy. The chassis and engine were basically unmodified 289 Cobra pieces ordered direct from Shelby. 3. Changes to the Jeep lineup were few for '65, but new for that year's CJ was a 225-cid/165-hp V-6 offered as an optional step up from the venerable Hurricane four-cylinder. The "new" six-cylinder engine was essentially a Buick design that had been purchased by Kaiser. 4, 5. King Midgets like this dolled-up example used a rear-mounted, single-cylinder Wisconsin engine. The 9.25-hp powerplant provided adequate performance and 50-75 mpg economy, aided of course by the car's tiny 700-pound curb weight.

2

3

4

5

1

2

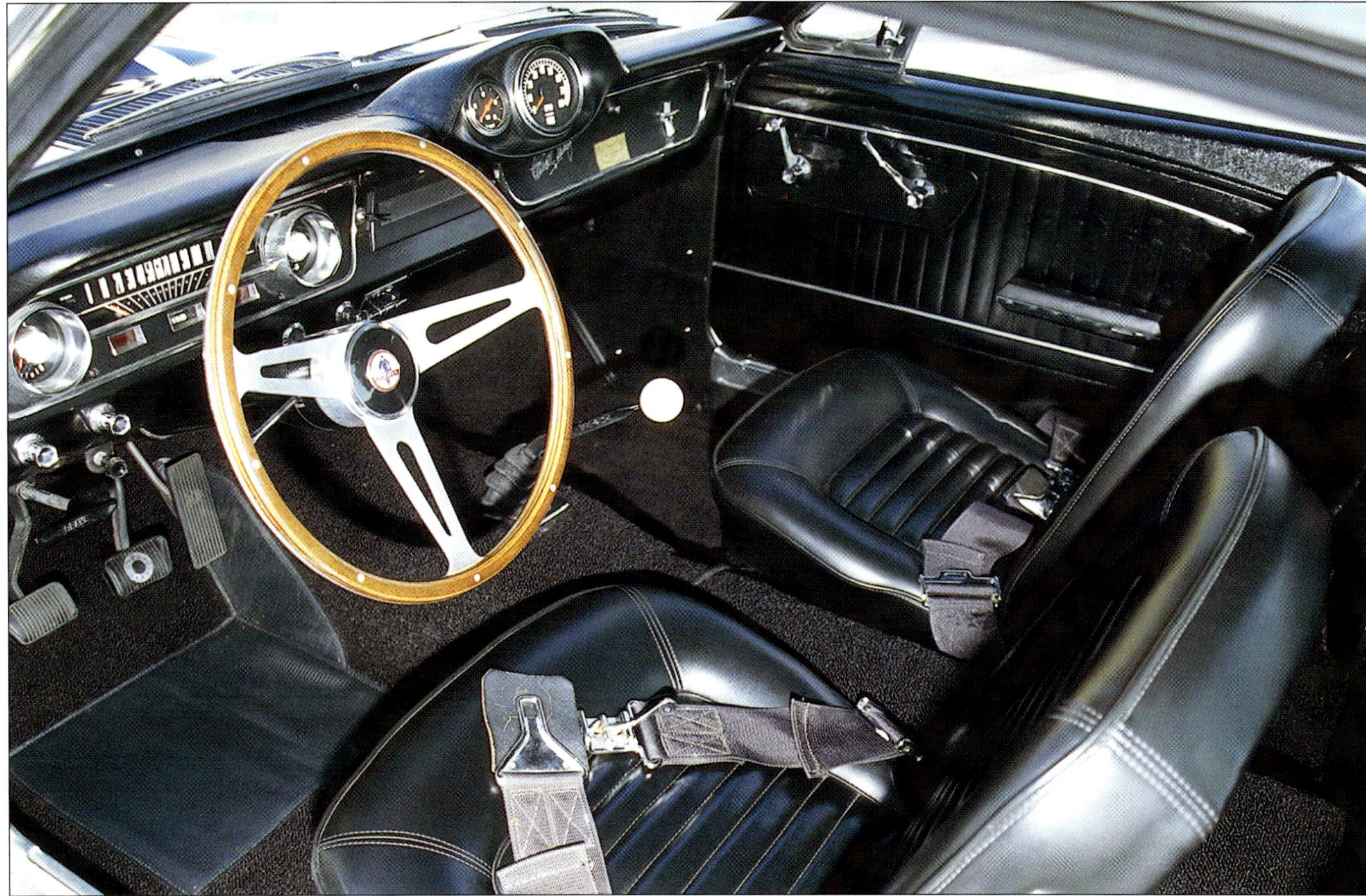
3

4

5

1, 2. Ford gave Carroll Shelby the nod to warm up the Mustang. He did so for '65 by creating the G.T. 350 (shown here) and the hotter, race-ready G.T. 350R. This G.T. 350 has the optional five-spoke Cragar wheels, offered in lieu of standard silver-painted steel wheels. From the outside, Rs could be easily identified by their lack of front and rear bumpers, and their unique wide-mouthed front valence. A total of 525 G.T. 350s were built for '65, along with 37 R models. 3. The street G.T. 350 included competition safety harness, and wood-rimmed Shelby steering wheel. The R version added a roll bar, but deleted the heater, glovebox door, and carpeting. Also, Rs had acrylic instead of glass rear and side windows. 4. The G.T. 350's businesslike cabin included this center-dashboard-mounted pod that held a tachometer and oil-pressure gauge. 5. Both G.T. 350 models used a solid-lifter 289-cid V-8. Shelby added headers, a high-rise aluminum intake manifold, and a 715-cfm Holley carburetor to boost output to 306 hp for street G.T. 350s (shown). In R tune, it made 350 hp via modified cylinder heads, hotter cam, and unmuffled exhaust. Racers could also order a Weber carbureted version that made 390 hp. Along with a stouter engine, all G.T. 350s had an aluminum-case Borg-Warner 4-speed transmission and Kelsey-Hayes front disc brakes. Visible here is Shelby's V-shaped "export brace" that ran between the shock towers and the firewall. Adding further stiffness to the chassis was a "Monte Carlo" bar running across the engine, connecting both fenders. The G.T. 350R was an overwhelming success on the track, with Jerry Titus taking the 1965 SCCA B-Production championship in one. However, the '65s would prove to be the purest of these pumped-up ponies; at Ford's request, Shelby toned down his G.T.s more with each model year that followed.

1

1, 2. Shelby's hot little Cobra sports car got even meaner in '65, with the introduction of the 427 version. From the outside, the 427 Cobra looked similar to its 289 forebear, but was in fact a rather different car that used a stronger frame; coil- instead of leaf-spring suspension; and a body that was shorter, wider, and taller. 3. The 427 Cobra's interior was much the same as the spartan cockpit of the 289 version. But racers probably didn't notice—they were likely too busy trying to control the big-engine car, which was by most accounts a real handful because of its brutal power and more front-heavy weight bias. Its 427-cid "FE" series big-block V-8 is said to have produced around 470-490 hp. Unfortunately, the car's obvious potential on the track was stunted by rule changes that favored smaller-engined cars. 4. Also part of the 427 Cobra were Halibrand racing wheels instead of the 289's wire wheels.

2

3

4

1965
1965
1965

INDEX